Cambridge Latin Course

Book I

Student Study Book

FOURTH EDITION

CAMBRIDGE UNIVERSITY PRESS

Cambridge, New York, Melbourne, Madrid, Cape Town, Singapore, São Paulo

Cambridge University Press
The Edinburgh Building, Cambridge CB2 8RU, UK

www.cambridge.org
Information on this title: www.cambridge.org/9780521685917

© University of Cambridge School Classics Project 1992, 1999, 2007

First published by the University of Cambridge School Classics Project
as *Independent Learning Manual Book I* 1992
Second edition 1999
Fourth edition 2007

Printed in the United Kingdom at the University Press, Cambridge

A catalogue record for this publication is available from the British Library

ISBN 978-0-521-68591-7 paperback

Preface

This *Student Study Book* is designed to be used in conjunction with Book I of the *Cambridge Latin Course* (ISBN 978-0-521-63543-1). It is intended for use by students in the following situations:

- students learning Latin on their own
- students on short courses who have to do much of the work on their own
- students being taught privately and requiring additional support material
- students who are catching up after illness or a change of schools
- students working ahead of the rest of the group
- teachers who wish to set cover work for a class
- classes in which independent learning is encouraged
- classes containing groups of students working at different levels.

An *Answer Key* is also available (ISBN 978-0-521-68592-4), as are online resources and e-tutor support (see page v).

The *Student Study Books* are re-workings of the earlier *Independent Learning Manuals*. In the creation of the original materials we benefited greatly from the advice and help of many teachers and students. In particular we should like to thank the following: Julien Melville for generously allowing us to make use of his own materials; Richard Woff, Neil Williams, Eileen Emmett, Betty Munday, Alex Nightingale and Wilf O'Neill for reading the draft materials and making many helpful suggestions and criticisms; Helen Vicat, whose ideas for pictures and skill in executing them have enlivened several pages; Helen Forte for her talented and witty artwork; Jean Groombridge; Christine Spillane; Joan Wootten; Jill Dalladay, for her suggestions for comprehension questions and exercises; Roger Dalladay, for his notes on the illustrations; Christine Simister, who pioneered the use of independent learning materials with the *Cambridge Latin Course*.

We are grateful to the following teachers and students who trialled the materials: Lucy Harrow and students at St Teresa's School, Dorking; Neil Williams' students at South Park Sixth Form College, Middlesbrough; David Karsten and students at Ranelagh School, Bracknell; Marian Small and students at St Margaret's School, Bushey; Jean Hubbard and her students at Banbury Community Education Council and Pat Story and her students at Coleridge Community College, Cambridge.

Finally, we should like to thank Betty Munday and Margaret Widdess for much detailed and demanding work; Debbie James for her meticulous reading of the texts; Maire Collins for designing and setting the original texts with such patience, care and ingenuity; and Jean Hubbard and Pat Story for all their work in developing, creating and editing the original *Independent Learning Manuals*. To these and all our other helpers we are much indebted.

Cambridge School Classics Project
July 2006

Introduction

Welcome to the *Cambridge Latin Course*. We hope you will enjoy learning Latin and finding out about the lives of people in different parts of the Roman Empire.

What you need to begin

The *Cambridge Latin Course Book I*, Fourth Edition.

If possible, you should have the *Cambridge Latin Course Worksheet Masters for Book I*. These are additional exercises on language points, word derivations and the background sections on Pompeii.

If you are working on your own without a teacher to mark your work, you will need the *Student Study Book I: Answer Key*.

These books are obtainable from Cambridge University Press.

Online resources

All the stories in *Cambridge Latin Course Book I* are available online in 'exploring' format. This allows you to click any word and see the vocabulary definition for that word instantly. You will also find interactive comprehensions, activities for practising grammar and many carefully selected weblinks for each Stage of the Book. All the resources are available free of charge at www.CambridgeSCP.com.

E-tutor support

If you would like tutored support through the Book, we can provide you with a distance e-tutor and study guide. You may begin your course whenever you choose and study at whatever pace suits you – your tutor will be on hand to help you for up to 40 weeks. All you need is a computer with an internet connection and an email account. For more information, please visit www.CambridgeSCP.com.

How the Course is designed

First, have a quick look through the *Cambridge Latin Course Book I* which is set in Pompeii. You will see that it is divided into 12 Stages, which have roughly the same layout.

Now look in detail at Stage 1. It starts on pp. 1 and 2 with pictures of Caecilius, a historical character from Pompeii. On the following pages you will see a series of pictures with sentences below them. These are called **Model sentences** and they introduce you to new points in the language. They also provide you with information about the theme of the Stage and introduce the other characters, mostly fictional.

On page 6 there is a story entitled **Cerberus**; usually there are two or more stories in a Stage. On page 7 the section called **About the language** explains a language point and the one called **Practising the language** contains revision exercises.

On pages 8–13 there are sections in English which give you further information about Caecilius, his wife Metella and houses in Pompeii. Every Stage has an English section which tells you more about life in Pompeii.

On the last page of Stage 1 and every other Stage is the **Vocabulary checklist** which contains words you have already met and which you need to learn.

At the end of the book is a **Vocabulary** which contains all the words in Book I.

The pictures

You will have noticed that there are a great many pictures in Book I.

The line drawings that accompany the **Model sentences** will help you to understand the meaning of the sentences and the new points in the language. They will also show you some of the activities of Caecilius, his family and the people in Pompeii and give you an idea of what Pompeii looked like before the eruption of Vesuvius.

Most of the colour photographs show the streets, buildings and objects that have been excavated in Pompeii. Like the drawings, they illustrate what is written in the Latin stories and the sections in English and will give you a vivid sense of what it was like to live in Pompeii.

How to use this Student Study Book

If you turn to page 1, you will find instructions for working through Stage 1. This book follows the same headings as those in the textbook and gives page references, e.g. **Model sentences p**p. 3–5.

Start working through the material in the order given in this book which is sometimes different from that in the textbook. This is to give you more variety.

> You will occasionally see instructions in smaller print in a box like this. These are for activities you can miss out if you are short of time.

You may wish to use an exercise book for your answers. Although there is space in this book for some shorter answers, there is not space for answers to every exercise.

How to check your answers

Check

This sign tells you when to check your answers. You do this by using the separate *Answer Key* if you do not have a teacher to help you.

How to learn efficiently

It is better to have several short sessions a week than one or two long ones. If you have only one or two long sessions in school, try to find short periods of time (even 10 minutes) in between to revise what you have learnt. This is particularly important when learning vocabulary or grammar.

Use active learning methods whenever possible; for example, in learning vocabulary, learn a few words and their meanings; then cover up the English meanings and give yourself a mini-test; better still, ask someone to test you. Then learn the next batch and give yourself another test.

How to keep track of your progress

You will find a **Progress record** at the end of each Stage in this book. You can use it to tick off work as you do it and again when you revise. There is also a space for any problems you would like to ask your teacher about.

How to pronounce Latin

The best way to learn to pronounce Latin is to listen to a teacher reading from the textbook and then imitate him or her.

Both in the textbook and in this book you will see that many Latin words have marks over some of the vowels. This is to help you to remember that those vowels have a long sound; e.g. ā in **māter** is pronounced like the *a* in *father*.

There is a **Short guide to the pronunciation of Latin** on p. 80.

Stage 1 Caecilius

Stage 1 introduces you to Caecilius and some of the members of his household. The drawing of Caecilius is based on the bronze head shown on the cover and p. 9 of your textbook. The head was found in Caecilius' villa, but no one really knows whether this is a portrait of Caecilius himself or an earlier member of his family. Notice the wart on his chin: people then often wanted a realistic likeness of themselves rather than one that flattered them.

Model sentences pp. 3–5

p. 3   Here is Caecilius and five members of the household: Metella, Quintus, Clemens, Grumio and Cerberus. If possible, listen to the sentences read by your teacher. Look at the pictures and work out who everyone is. Use the **Vocabulary** on p. 6 to check if necessary.

p. 4   Study the sentences. Work out where everyone is, using the pictures and **Vocabulary** to help you.

p. 5   Study the sentences. The first one of each pair tells you again where each member of the family is; the second what he or she is doing. Find this out, again using the pictures and **Vocabulary**.

Check

Check your work with your teacher or use the *Answer Key*.
Practise reading the Latin sentences aloud.

Houses in Pompeii pp. 10–13

1   Read the section. As you come to the Latin names for the various parts of the house, find out where they are by looking at the plan on p. 11. Study the photograph on p. 11 and answer the question below it.

2   When you have read the section and studied the pictures and their captions, look again at the large picture on p. 12. You are viewing the inside of the house from the entrance hall right through to the garden at the back, as a visitor in Roman times would have done. What do you think the owner wanted you to feel?

Check

Roman house quiz

In this picture you are looking into the atrium from the **tablīnum** (*study*) marked D. Can you identify the other features?

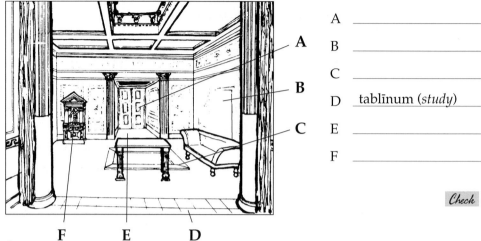

A _____

B _____

C _____

D ___tablīnum (study)___

E _____

F _____

Check

Cerberus p. 6

Read the story and work out its meaning, using the vocabulary on the right-hand side of the page if necessary.

Notice that:

1. There is no word for *a* or *the* in the sentences. For example, **coquus est in culīnā** can mean *A cook is in the kitchen* or *The cook is in the kitchen*. The story will help you to decide whether it is better to say *a* or *the*.

2. There are no capital letters at the beginning of the Latin sentences, except for names.

Check

Picture

It was quite common to have a mosaic of a watchdog just inside the front door, which was usually kept open during the day. Caecilius' dog looks very relaxed. Look at p. 177 where you will find a fiercer animal with the inscription **cavē canem**, *Beware of the dog*.

About the language p. 7

Read carefully. Note the kind of sentence where the order of words is different from English.

Practising the language p. 7

Ex. 1 Work out the exercise in your head.

Ex. 2 Write out as instructed in the book.

Check

Caecilius and Metella pp. 8–10

Read these sections and study the map and pictures.

1 How would the position of Pompeii on the coast have been an advantage to Caecilius as a businessman? (Note that the map shows the modern position of Pompeii some distance from the sea.)

2 What other evidence is there in the rest of this Stage that Caecilius was a wealthy man?

3 The name **Iucundus** means *pleasant*. Does your name have a meaning? Do you know where it comes from? For example, *George*, originally a Greek name, means *farmer*; *Shanti*, an Indian girl's name, means *peace*.

4 Metella would be responsible for organising the work of a large number of domestic slaves. From what you have read in this Stage what kinds of work would they have to do?

5 Look at the pictures of women's hairstyles on p. 10. Which hairstyle is the one most like Metella's?

 Check

Vocabulary checklist 1 p. 14

Learn the checklist. Test that you know the meanings of the Latin words by covering up the English.

You will have noticed that several English words are derived from the Latin words you have met in this Stage. If you know Latin you can often guess the meaning of words in English or other modern languages. For example:

1 What kind of job would you have if it was

sedentary? _____

horticultural? _____

labouring? _____

2 What kind of person would you be if you were

servile? _____

maternal? _____

Check

Progress record   Textbook pp. 1–14   Student Study Book pp. 1–3

Stage 1 Caecilius	Done	Revised	Any problems?
Model sentences			
Houses in Pompeii			
Roman house quiz			
Cerberus			
About the language			
Practising the language			
Caecilius and Metella			
Vocabulary checklist 1			

Stage 2 in vīllā

In this Stage a friend visits Caecilius. In the picture
Caecilius is waiting for his friend to arrive.

1   Where is Caecilius waiting?

2   How do you know?

3   To the right of the far opening is a bronze object
    mounted on a stone base. Can you suggest what
    the object is?

Check

Picture p. 15

This is the first time you have had a picture of this type of room. What is it? Can
you remember its Latin name? The walls are painted with theatre scenes which
were popular among the Pompeians.

Check

Model sentences pp. 16–19

Study the Latin sentences and find out what happens when the friend visits
Caecilius. Use the pictures and the new words below to help you. You can
probably guess the other new words.

cibus	*food*	parātus	*ready*	gustat	*tastes*
laudat	*praises*	vocat	*calls*		

You will notice that some words which you had in Stage 1 have a different
spelling here (e.g. **Caecilius** is sometimes spelt **Caecilium**). Do not worry about this
as the words still have the same meaning in English. The reason for the change
will be explained later. *Check*

Look again at the pictures and answer the questions below. If you are in a
group, you could discuss the questions together.

pp. 16–17   1   How is the friend's greeting to Clemens different from his greeting to the rest
            of the household? Why do you think it is different?

            2   Do you think the dog is pleased to see the friend or not? How does the picture
            confirm your answer?

pp. 18–19   3   Write down THREE details about food or cooking shown in any of the pictures
            which you consider different from modern times.

Check

mercātor p. 20

Read lines 1–6. Using the vocabulary, work out the meaning in your head.

Here is an English translation of these lines. Compare it with the Latin and underline the sentences where there is a difference in the order of the words.

A friend is visiting Caecilius. The friend is a merchant. The merchant enters the house. Clemens is in the atrium. Clemens greets the merchant. Caecilius is in the study. Caecilius is counting money. Caecilius is a banker. The friend enters the study. Caecilius gets up.

'Hello!' Caecilius greets the merchant.

'Hello!' the merchant replies.

Now write your own translation of the rest of this story.

Check

Daily life pp. 23–5

Read this section and answer these questions.

1 Look at the drawings of Caecilius and Metella in this Stage. How similar are their clothes to those of the male and female statues on pp. 10 and 23?

2 Study the picture at the bottom of p. 23. Can you see what the three figures are holding or carrying? Can you guess the purpose of the curved object on the right?

3 Make a diary of a day in the life of Caecilius and the same for Metella. You may find it helpful to re-read the background section on Caecilius and Metella in Stage 1, pp. 8–10. If you are in a group, some of you could take Caecilius and others Metella; then compare.

4 In what ways were the times of meals and eating habits of Caecilius and his household different from modern times? Do you find any similarities at all?

5 Would you have enjoyed a Roman dinner as described on pp. 24–5? Give your reasons. Have you ever eaten a similar meal? If so, what did you have?

6 What foods that we eat now were not available in Roman times? Would you say that Caecilius and his family had a healthy diet? Give reasons for your answer.

Check

in triclīniō p. 20

Read this story about the dinner Caecilius gave to his friend and answer the questions.

1 Which TWO people come into the dining-room and what is each of them carrying?

2 In line 4 which Latin word does Caecilius use to praise the food?

3 **mercātor cēnam laudat** (line 5). Why does the merchant praise the meal? Is he merely being polite?

4 Read again lines 7–9 and, for each of the pictures below, write out the Latin sentence which describes what is happening.

5 In line 10 why do you think Grumio comes back into the dining-room?

6 What FOUR things does Grumio do after he comes back?

7 Why does Caecilius not see Grumio?

8 **coquus in triclīniō magnificē cēnat**. Why would Caecilius consider that Grumio's action here is wrong?

9 Why, at the end of the story, is Grumio very happy?

Check

About the language p. 21

Read carefully the explanation for the different forms of the same noun, which you have been meeting in this Stage. Aim to recognise as soon as possible the **nominative** and **accusative** forms and to understand why they are used.

The accusative generally ends in the letter **m**.

1 Translate these two sentences:

Clēmēns mēnsam portat.

māter fīlium audit.

Who is performing the action in these two sentences?

What case is used?

2 Translate these two sentences:

ancilla **culīnam** intrat.

mercātor in triclīniō cēnat.

What are the cases of the nouns in **bold type**?

Check

Practising the language p. 22

Ex. 1 Work out the sentences in your head.

Ex. 2 Write out this exercise which tests word meaning but also includes the nominative and accusative forms.

Ex. 3 **amīcus** You should be able to read and understand this story without much difficulty. There is no need to write it out. *Check*

Vocabulary checklist 2 p. 26

Learn the checklist.

1 What sort of person would you be if you were *amiable*?

2 How do soldiers greet each other?

3 What would you expect your teacher to do if you did something *laudable*?

4 Solve these jumbled Latin words which are included in the list you have just learned. Try to work without looking up, aiming to spell the Latin words correctly.

	Latin word	Meaning		Latin word	Meaning
acne			timrod		
ranitt			ouqequ		
troracem			taladu		
atelsu			bisuc		

5 Find EIGHT Latin words, all denoting people, hidden in this square. The words go either straight across or straight down. Give their meaning.

You have learnt all these words in Stages 1 and 2.

											Latin word	Meaning
C	L	I	C	O	Q	U	U	S		1	_____	_____
U	N	A	P	B	I	F	D	T				
A	P	A	T	E	R	I	O	M		2	_____	_____
N	U	A	V	I	D	L	M	A				
C	S	M	G	U	S	I	I	T		3	_____	_____
I	T	I	A	E	T	U	N	E		4	_____	_____
L	G	C	P	V	A	S	U	R		5	_____	_____
L	M	U	L	C	V	T	S	E		6	_____	_____
A	O	S	S	E	R	V	U	S		7	_____	_____
										8	_____	_____

Check

Language test

Before going on to Stage 3 make sure that you understand the language work of Stages 1 and 2 by doing this test. Do the test without referring to your book.

1 Complete each sentence with the correct nominative or accusative case. Then translate each sentence into English.

    a amīcus _____ vīsitat. (Caecilius, Caecilium)

    b dominus _____ laudat. (ancilla, ancillam)

    c _____ hortum intrat. (Metella, Metellam)

    d Quīntus _____ salūtat. (pater, patrem)

    e _____ cēnam cōnsūmit. (mercātor, mercātōrem)

2 From the following passage pick out FOUR different nominatives and FOUR different accusatives. Write them in the table.

amīcus Caecilium vīsitat. amīcus est mercātor. mercātor vīllam intrat. Clēmēns est in ātriō. Clēmēns mercātōrem salūtat. Caecilius est in tablīnō. Caecilius pecūniam numerat. amīcus tablīnum intrat. Caecilius surgit.

Nominative	Accusative

3 Read this story about Caecilius and his friend's peacock. Fill in the gaps with suitable words from the box below. Use each word only once. Then translate the whole story and answer the question at the end.

Caecilius et pāvō

est	Caecilium	clāmat
in hortō	coquum	intrat
coquus	vīllam	laudat

Caecilius amīcum vīsitat. Caecilius _____ intrat. amīcus est in hortō. pāvō quoque est _____. amīcus _____ salūtat. pāvō Caecilium videt. Caecilius pāvōnem nōn dēlectat. pāvō _____ īrātus. pāvō Caecilium agitat (*chases*).

    Caecilius culīnam _____. coquus in culīnā labōrat. _____ cēnam coquit. pāvō quoque culīnam intrat. pāvō _____ videt. pāvō est anxius. coquus pāvōnem vituperat.

    'pestis! furcifer!' coquus _____ . pāvō exit. Caecilius est laetus. Caecilius coquum _____ .

Why do you think the cook had such an effect on the peacock?

Check

If you had any problems, read again **About the language** p. 21 or ask your teacher.

Progress record   Textbook pp. 15–26   Student Study Book pp. 5–9

Stage 2 in vīllā	Done	Revised	Any problems?
Model sentences			
mercātor			
Daily life			
in triclīniō			
About the language			
Practising the language			
Vocabulary checklist 2			
Language test			

Stage 3 negōtium

In this Stage our attention turns from Caecilius at home to Caecilius at work. We meet the three people pictured on the right and find out what jobs they do and what activities go on in the town.

There is no new language point in Stage 3 and therefore no model sentences. The stories will help you to revise the points you have already met and they will also build up your knowledge of vocabulary.

Picture p. 27

This wall-painting of an unknown harbour reminds us of the port at Pompeii although that would have been more commercial and less picturesque than the one in the picture. Notice the colonnades on the left with marble ornaments hanging between the columns, the fortifications on the right and the pillars with statues of famous citizens on top. A fisherman with his rod is perched on the rock in the foreground.

in forō p. 28

The forum was the large open space in Pompeii where markets were held and business was carried on.

Read the story and work out the meaning without writing a translation. Then do the following exercise.

1   Write in the table the names and occupations of the FOUR people in the story who are in the forum.

Person	Occupation

2   Look at the drawing on p. 28. Can you identify these four people?

3   One of the people is angry. Who is he and why is he angry?

4   From lines 1–4 pick out THREE nouns in the nominative case and THREE in the accusative case. Write them in the table.

Nominative	Accusative

5   Look at the following sentences:

    a   vēnālīcius mercātōrem exspectat.

    b   mercātor vēnālīcium exspectat.

    What is the difference in the meaning?

Check

pictor p. 29

Read the story and work out the meaning.

Most of the family are at home when Celer arrives at the house. What do each of them do or not do in connection with Celer? Write down what happens in the table below.

Character	Reaction to Celer
Clemens	
Cerberus	
Quintus	
Metella	
Caecilius	

Celer paints a picture of the hero Hercules fighting a lion. This was one of the twelve tests or labours that this hero had to perform. Label the picture on the right with suitable words or phrases from lines 8–11.
Check

Celer would paint his picture of Hercules on a wall that had been prepared with three coats of fine polished plaster. He painted quickly on the plaster while it was still wet, so that the colours were absorbed into the surface. The paints were made from powdered minerals mixed with egg or honey and Celer would make these up as required.

Wall-paintings of scenes from myths and legends were popular in Pompeii, as were many other subjects. You can get an idea of the variety by looking at the wall-paintings at the bottom of p. 29 and the many other examples in Book I. For an impression of what a complete room looked like, turn back to p. 15.

tōnsor p. 30

Read the story and then write down the answers to the questions.
Check

vēnālīcius p. 31

Read lines 1–10 and work out the meaning. Then answer the following questions. You need not write them down. If you are in a group, you could discuss them orally.

1 Why does Caecilius go to the harbour?

2 **Syphāx rīdet** (line 6). Why do you think Syphax does this?

3 Why do you think Caecilius is dissatisfied (lines 7–8)?

4 **'vīnum!' clāmat Syphāx** (line 9). Why do you think Syphax calls for wine to be served to Caecilius at this point?

Read lines 11–17 and write out a translation of them. Without looking at the story again, answer the following questions.

5 What do you think of Caecilius' behaviour in this story?

6 Why does Metella not like Melissa? Do you sympathise with Metella?

Check

Practising the language p. 33

Ex. 1 Do the first three sentences in your head; write out **d** and **e**.

Ex. 2 This exercise tests nominative and accusative forms. Write out the sentences and translate them.

Check

If you made any mistakes, revise the use of the nominative and accusative on p. 21.

About the language p. 32

You have already learnt the difference between the nominative and accusative cases. This note shows you how the nominatives and accusatives you have met can be divided into three groups or declensions. Read the note carefully.

Further exercise Arrange the following words in their declensions in the table below.

cēnam   dominus   nāvem   leō   taberna   coquum   iānua   senem   cibum

First declension			
Second declension			
Third declension			

Check

The town of Pompeii pp. 33–7

If you are in a group, you could divide up the questions between you.
Read pp. 33–4 and look at the town plan.

1 What was the size of Pompeii? Is this smaller or larger than the place where you live?

2 What did the town have to protect it from an enemy? It was unlikely that Pompeii would be attacked at this time. Can you think why?

3 How would you describe the pattern of streets? Do you know of any more recent town planned like this?

4 Study the plan on p. 34. Suppose Syphax on his next trip to Pompeii wanted to meet Caecilius again. By which gate would he enter the town? What directions to Caecilius' house would you give him? Remember that the street names on the plan are modern inventions.

Now study the text and pictures on pp. 35–7.

5 You have already met a painter, a barber and a slave-dealer in this Stage. This section provides evidence for several other trades. Make a list of them.

6 People of many nationalities visited or lived in Pompeii. Of the characters you have met in this Stage Celer has a Latin name and might have been one of the group of wall-painters who lived in or near Pompeii. Pantagathus has a Greek name; he may have been descended from a Greek family that came to live in Pompeii a long time before.

   Where do you think Syphax and Melissa might have come from? Why? The story on p. 31 will help you.

7 How did the Pompeians spend their leisure time? Remember to study the pictures and plan as well as the text.

Vocabulary checklist 3 p. 38

Learn the checklist.

1 Without looking at the checklist, pick out from the box every action that can be done silently. You may have doubts about one or two.

bibit	circumspectat
exspectat	clāmat
exit	portat
respondet	rīdet
videt	surgit

2 The Latin letter **i** sometimes appears in English derivations as the letter **j**. With which word in the checklist is the word *January* connected? What is the link between them?

Language test

1 Complete the words in the following pairs of sentences with the correct form of the nominative or accusative and translate.

    a servus in hortō labōrat.

        Metella serv_____ laudat.

    b canis in viā sedet.

        amīcus can_____ salūtat.

    c leō est in pictūrā.

        Caecilius leōn_____ spectat.

    d Caecilius ancillam videt.

        ancill_____ rīdet.

    e mercātor vēnālīcium exspectat.

        vēnālīci_____ forum intrat.

2 Here is a list of words in the nominative or accusative case. Decide which of the three declensions or groups each word belongs to and label it 1, 2 or 3. The first two are done for you.

servus	2	tōnsōrem	
taberna	1	iānuam	
fīlium		senex	
mēnsa		dominus	
nāvem		cēnam	
patrem		cibus	

Check

If you had any problems, read again **About the language** p. 32 or ask your teacher.

Progress record   Textbook pp. 27–38   Student Study Book pp. 11–15

Stage 3 negōtium	Done	Revised	Any problems?
in forō			
pictor			
tōnsor			
vēnālīcius			
Practising the language			
About the language			
The town of Pompeii			
Vocabulary checklist 3			
Language test			

Stage 4 in forō

In Stage 4, the scene is set again in the forum. The stories show the kind of problem which Caecilius would meet in his business.

Look at this picture of the forum. Normally it would have been very busy and crowded with people. Pick out from the picture THREE features which you consider interesting. If you are in a group, discuss the points you have each chosen. If you have any queries you may find the answers on pp. 48–51.

Check

Picture p. 39

This shows the forum from the opposite direction to the drawing above. You can see part of the Temple of Jupiter on the right of the photograph. What do you think is the purpose of the two stone blocks in the foreground?

Check

Model sentences pp. 40–2

In these sentences you will find out how the Pompeians talked about themselves and asked questions.

p. 40   **Sentences 1** Grumio is describing who he is and what he is doing. What is he saying about himself?

Sentences 2–6 are about other characters, but follow the same pattern.

p. 41   **Sentences 7–12** Quintus asks various characters what they are doing. What questions does he put to them? What are their answers?

p. 42   **Sentences 13–15** Metella asks three characters who they are. What is her question to each of them? What are their answers?

When you have read all the sentences on pp. 40–2, write down the words the characters keep on using. What are their meanings?

Check

Picture p. 43

Can you find this corner of the forum in the drawing at the top of this page? Why would the colonnade be a desirable feature of the forum?

Check

Hermogenēs p. 43

Read the story. Write out a translation of lines 1–9, then work out the meaning of the rest of the story (lines 10–16) and answer these questions.

1 **cēram, ānulum** (lines 10–11). What are these objects and who has them? See pp. 44 and 47 for photographs of the objects.

2 In line 12 what does Hermogenes do with these objects? Why do you suppose he does this?

3 What does Hermogenes do as soon as he receives the money? Do you think that Caecilius would be worried by this?

4 How does the story end?

Caecilius Hermogenem ad basilicam vocat.

About the language p. 45

Read p. 45, noting the new forms. Work out the sentences in paragraph 5. You need not write out a translation of sentences **a–d**, but write out the rest, taking particular care with **g** and **h**.

Further exercise

Here are some actions where the person doing them has been left out. Fill in the table as appropriate with either **ego** or **tū** or **servus** and write down the translation. The first one is done for you.

Person	Translation	Person	Translation
servus currit	The slave is running	_____ habeō	
_____ venīs		_____ vocat	
_____ labōrō		_____ vidēs	

in basilicā p. 44

Read the play and work out the meaning.

1 Read the statements below. Say whether each statement is TRUE or FALSE. If you are in a group, work through the statements orally.

   a Caecilius is a Roman citizen.

   b Caecilius is in the forum every day.

   c The judge says Caecilius is a liar.

   d Hermogenes never comes to the forum.

   e Hermogenes denies that he owes any money.

   f Hermogenes has a friend in court.

   g Hermogenes asks Caecilius for proof.

   h Caecilius tells the judge to press his seal on the wax tablet.

   i Hermogenes tries to hide the evidence.

   j Hermogenes is finally acquitted from lack of evidence.

2 Look at the pictures of law courts on pp. 46–7. Where would Caecilius, Hermogenes and his friend be standing during the trial?

Check

If you are in a group, you may like to act the play and, if possible, record yourselves.

Practising the language pp. 46–7

Ex. 1 Work out the meaning of the sentences in **a–f**. Then write out your answers for **g–j**.

Check

Ex. 2 Grumiō et leō

Read the story carefully and work out what happens. The words in the list below could be used to describe the characters in the story. Say which character you would describe by each word and give a reason based on the story.

Description	Character	Reason
sensible		
artistic		
drunk		
witty		
frightened		

Check

The forum pp. 48–51

Read the information on these pages and study the pictures.

1 What was the size of the forum? Pace out the measurements on your school field.

2 Identify the buildings on the plan below by numbering them as in the key. See how much you can do without looking at the aerial view on p. 51.

3 At the side of each building in the key can you enter an equivalent one in your area? This question and the next are good ones to discuss with other members of your group.

4 In your area are the equivalent buildings close together or far apart? Why are they situated like that?

Ground plan of forum

1 Temple of Jupiter

2 Market hall

3 Temple of the Lares of Pompeii

4 Temple of the Emperors

5 Eumachia's Clothworkers' Guildhall

6 Polling station

7 Municipal offices

8 Basilica

9 Temple of Apollo

10 Table of weights and measures

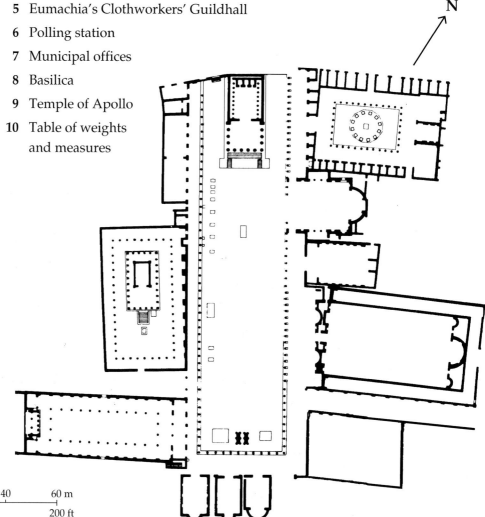

```
      20        40      60 m
0 ├────────┼────────┼────────┤
        100          200 ft
```

Vocabulary checklist 4 p. 52

Learn the checklist.

1 Who do you think would conduct a judicial inquiry into something that has happened?

2 Many Latin words connected with questions begin with the letter **q**. What are the meanings of **quis** and **quaerit**?

3 When Hermogenes first met Caecilius he claimed to be *impecunious*. What does that mean?

4 If your work is said to be *satisfactory*, should you feel pleased? Give a reason for your answer.

5 What does it mean if we say someone has a *vocation* to be a doctor?

6 Short words in Latin are often the most difficult to remember. What do these mean: **sed**, **ēheu**, **agit**, **ē**, **cūr**?

 Check

Language test

1 Complete each sentence by inserting the correct word from the box below and then translate the sentence.

| ego | tū | poēta |

a _____ forum circumspectō.

b _____ in triclīniō dormit.

c _____ in viā stō.

d _____ magnam nāvem habēs.

e _____ ad vīllam ambulat.

2 Tick the word in brackets that completes the sentence and then translate the sentence.

a ego ancillam _____.
(vocō, vocās, vocat)

b māter ānulum _____.
(quaerō, quaeris, quaerit)

c tū pecūniam nōn _____.
(reddō, reddis, reddit)

d Grumiō cēnam _____.
(coquō, coquis, coquit)

e ego in cērā signum _____.
(videō, vidēs, videt)

f ego _____ perterritus.
(sum, es, est)

3 Translate the following sentences, looking carefully at each ending.

a respondeō.

b rīdēs.

c surgō.

d in culīnā labōrō.

e in ātriō sedēs.

Check

Progress record   Textbook pp. 39–52   Student Study Book pp. 17–21

Stage 4 in forō	Done	Revised	Any problems?
Model sentences			
Hermogenēs			
About the language			
in basilicā			
Practising the language			
The forum			
Vocabulary checklist 4			
Language test			

Stage 5 in theātrō

This Stage describes what might have happened in Pompeii when a company of travelling actors arrived to perform plays in the theatre at a festival. Masks like the one on the right were worn by actors. Pictures and carvings of masks were popular as decorations all over the Roman world; you will find several examples in this Stage. Actors wear masks in some countries today.

Picture p. 53

Part of a Pompeian wall-painting, showing Oceanus, a sea god. The unusual colour of his face is meant to represent the colour of the sea.

Model sentences pp. 54–7

pp. 54–5 The pictures show one of the streets near the theatre and some of the people and animals. Look at the pictures and study the sentences. You have not met the words **puella** and **puer** before but you will be able to guess their meanings from the pictures. You will find the sentences on the left of the page very easy and you should be able to understand those on the right with the help of the pictures.

What is the difference in meaning between the sentences on the left and their partners on the right? Write down the words which change.

Check

pp. 56–7 In the first picture you see the large theatre at Pompeii before the audience arrives. Some members of the audience are shown in the other pictures. Before translating the sentences, see if you can answer these questions about the theatre.

1 What do you think the seats were made of?

2 Where are the entrances for the audience?

3 How would you describe the back of the stage?

4 This was an open-air theatre. What protection was given to the actors and the audience?

Now study the sentences and look at the pictures as before. The following words and phrases are new, but easy to understand:

spectātor	āctor	in scaenā
fēmina	iuvenis	plaudit

What is the difference in each pair of pictures? Write down the words which change.

Check

āctōrēs p. 58

This story tells you about the day the actors came to town. Read the story and work out the meaning. Then answer the following questions.

1 What is special about this day from the point of view of

   a the slaves

   b the old men

   c the merchants?

2 Where is everybody going?

3 The second paragraph mentions three types of people who normally work elsewhere but who are flocking to Pompeii today. Who are they?

4 What job has Priscus taken on?

5 Who are Actius and Sorex?

6 Which member of Caecilius' household is **not** going to the theatre? Can you suggest a reason?

7 How would you describe the atmosphere in Pompeii on this particular day? Have you experienced anything similar in the place where you live?

Check

Picture p. 58

These statues of actors wearing their masks were once brightly coloured. Can you tell which is the male character and which the female? Now turn to the wall-painting of an actor on p. 60. Why do you think he is looking so intently at his mask?

Check

About the language 1 pp. 59–60

1 Read paragraphs 1–3 and note how the words change. Without looking again at paragraph 3, can you tell which of the following verbs are singular and which are plural?

    spectant; stat; plaudunt; audit.

2 Read paragraph 4. If you learn French you can see the similarities with Latin. For example:

    amīcus **est** in theātrō. amīcī **sunt** in theātrō.

    L'ami *est* dans le théâtre. Les amis *sont* dans le théâtre.

How has the pronunciation changed?

Check

Poppaea p. 61

This play introduces two new characters: Lucrio, an old man, and his young slave-girl, Poppaea. The action takes place in their villa as the Pompeians swarm along the streets to the theatre. Read the play and work out the meaning.

Check

If you are in a group you can read the play in parts. You will need three actors to take the parts of Lucrio, Poppaea and the friend, and someone to read the stage direction at the beginning. Everyone else can join in as **agricolae** and **pueri**.

When you have read the play, discuss the behaviour of Lucrio and Poppaea. You may like to perform the play in Latin or write out a script for acting it in English.

About the language 2 p. 62

Read paragraph 1. Note again that if a sentence changes from singular to plural, TWO words have to change; e.g. in the first example, **puella** becomes **puellae** and **rīdet** becomes **rīdent**.

Read paragraphs 2, 3 and 4 then translate the sentences in paragraph 5.

Further exercise Arrange the following nominatives in the columns headed singular and plural:

ancilla   nautae   senēs   āctor   puerī   iuvenis   fēmina   spectātōrēs

Nominative singular		Nominative plural	

Now make a sentence by selecting suitable singular and plural words from the box below and putting them in the blank spaces next to each nominative. Use each word only once.

rīdet   plaudunt   currunt   clāmant   labōrat   intrat   dormiunt   adest

If you are in a group you could give your sentences to someone else to check and translate.

Check

The theatre at Pompeii pp. 64–7

pp. 64–6 1 Read the text on pp. 64–6 and study the pictures.

   a Can you think of a modern-day entertainment or festival which involves the whole community? If not, what would be the nearest equivalent?

   b Compare the photograph of the large theatre at Pompeii with the reconstruction on p. 56. Which parts of the theatre are well preserved? How do we know that the reconstruction is probably accurate?

pp. 66–7 2 Read the text entitled *The comedies of Plautus* and study the accompanying pictures.

   a In pictures 1–4 on p. 67, how do the masks indicate the different types of character in a comedy?

   b Masks were also worn by actors in serious plays. Look at the masks on p. 23 of this book and p. 60 of the textbook. How do they differ from most of those worn by the comic actors on pp. 66–7?

    Check

Further activities 1 Worksheet Master 5.6 is a scene from a comedy by Plautus, which you can act.

   2 Draw and colour a theatrical mask or make one. Worksheet Master 5.7 gives you templates of two masks and directions to make them.

Practising the language p. 63

Ex. 1 Write out the sentences and translate them.

Ex. 2 This exercise is not so straightforward as Ex.1. Write out the sentences and translate them.

Ex. 3 **in theātrō** As further revision of vocabulary and singular and plural sentences, read the story.

   The idea for this story came from the Roman playwright Terence. He tells us that the audience rushed out of the theatre when one of his plays was being performed to watch a tight-rope walker and boxing match.

   fūnambulus is made up of two Latin words, **fūnis** and **ambulō**. You know what **ambulō** means; guess what **fūnis** means. There is a picture of a tight-rope walker on p. 68.

   Check

Vocabulary checklist 5 p. 68

Learn the checklist.

1 What English word comes from the Latin for farmer?

2 Why do people who have been in accidents need *ambulances* and babies need *perambulators* (*prams*)?

3 Actors often go to an *audition*. Why is it called this?

4 What kind of people are *juveniles*?

5 What is an *optimist*?

6 What is a bus *station*?

7 If you are cycling along a road and come to an *urban* area, where are you?

Check

Language test

1 Complete the sentences by adding **-t** or **-nt** to the unfinished word. Translate the sentences.

  a agricolae in urbe ambula___.

  b fēmina puellam vide___.

  c amīcus fābulam specta___.

  d iuvenēs in theātrō sede___.

  e turba in viā sta___.

2 Complete each sentence with the right form of the noun from the brackets. Then translate the sentence.

  a _____ in theātrō clāmat. (puer, puerī)

  b _____ sunt in scaenā. (āctor, āctōrēs)

  c _____ per urbem currunt. (servī, servus)

  d _____ est in triclīniō. (mercātōrēs, mercātor)

  e _____ in viā dormiunt. (canis, canēs)

Check

Progress record   Textbook pp. 53–68   Student Study Book pp. 23–7

Stage 5 in theātrō	Done	Revised	Any problems?
Model sentences			
āctōrēs			
About the language 1			
Poppaea			
About the language 2			
The theatre at Pompeii			
Practising the language			
Vocabulary checklist 5			
Language test			

Stage 6 Fēlīx

You have now read several stories about the slaves in Caecilius' household and have seen how a new slave-girl was bought. In Stage 6 you meet an ex-slave called Felix and find out how slaves might be set free.

Picture p. 69

This stone relief may show a slave being set free at an official ceremony. This is explained later in the Stage.

Model sentences pp. 70–1

In Stages 1–5 the action in the stories has been presented in a lively way, as though the events were taking place now before your eyes, e.g. Stage 5 p. 58.

magna turba est in urbe.

A big crowd is in the city.

pāstōrēs dē monte veniunt.

Shepherds are coming down from the mountain.

But obviously the stories really refer to life in Pompeii over two thousand years ago.

In Stage 6 the events are presented as happening in the past. Study the sentences and work out the meaning. You may find it helpful, before starting the first sentence, to supply the Latin word **ōlim** meaning *long ago*.

These words in the sentences are new ones:

TODAY THE SUN IS SHINING
SO I AM PLEASED WITH LIFE . . .

subitō	*suddenly*
timēbat	*was afraid*
fortis	*brave*
superāvit	*overpowered*
vexābat	*was annoying, harassing*
pulsāvit	*hit*

 Check

BUT YESTERDAY IT WAS RAINING
AND I FELL IN A PUDDLE.

pugna p. 72

Read this story which is set in the forum. Then look below at the list of groups and individuals who were in the forum. By placing the correct letter in the spaces, match the statements to the characters.

Groups and individuals	Letter	Statements
Slaves and slave-girls		a were laughing.
Many bakers		b hurried to the fight.
A poet		c were buying food.
The Greek merchant		d was reciting.
The farmer		e were selling bread.
The Pompeians		f hit the Greek.
Clemens		g was demanding money.

Who won the fight? Why do you think that the Pompeians supported the farmer?

Check

Fēlīx p. 72

Read the story and work out the meaning. In the story the characters behave in certain ways. Can you suggest possible reasons for their behaviour? If you are working in a group, you could discuss your individual answers and your evidence for them.

Lines	Characters	Behaviour	Suggested reason
2–3	Clemens		
6–7	Caecilius and Metella		
8–9	Felix		
11–12	Grumio		

Check

Fēlīx et fūr p. 73

1 Read lines 1–8 and work out the meaning in your head.

2 Then read lines 9–19 and write out a translation, taking care to translate the new imperfect and perfect tenses correctly.

3 Read to the end of the story (lines 20–3).

4 Does this story explain anything in the previous story Fēlīx?

Check

About the language pp. 74–5

This language note explains how to describe events that took place in the past. You have seen these new verb forms in the **Model sentences** and in the stories on pp. 72–3.

1 Read paragraphs 1–3, noting the forms of the different tenses of the verb. Then test yourself by completing the following sentences and say whether each is imperfect or perfect.

Latin	English	Tense
poēta recitābat.	The poet _____.	
servī ambulābant.	The slaves _____.	
amīcus intrāvit.	The friend _____.	
mercātōrēs festīnāvērunt.	The merchants _____.	
Pompēiānī rīdēbant.	The Pompeians _____.	
Quīntus Fēlīcem salūtāvit.	Quintus _____ Felix.	
Clēmēns et Fēlix Grumiōnem excitāvērunt.	Clemens and Felix _____ Grumio.	

2 Read paragraph 4 and then give the Latin for the words in **bold type** in the story below.

One day Grumio and the other slaves **were** in the garden. On the kitchen table there **were** vegetables, sausages and fruit for dinner. Cerberus **was** by the door. Grumio came in. The sausages **were** no longer on the table! There **was** no one else in the kitchen, but Cerberus **was** sleepy and very happy.

3 Read paragraphs 5 and 6. State whether the verbs in **bold type** in the story below are imperfect or perfect.

Caecilius **was working** in the forum. A merchant **caught sight of** Caecilius and **greeted** him. While they **were discussing** business, a jackdaw **flew down** and **seized** a silver coin. The merchant **cursed** the jackdaw, but Caecilius **laughed**.

'What you **were telling** me', he **said** 'is worth much more than one silver coin.'

Check

Slaves and freedmen pp. 78–81

First read pp. 78–9, which are about slavery, and study the pictures. If you are working in a group, you could divide up the questions and discuss your answers.

1 Slaves did not possess the same rights as free people. Often, however, they did not seem to be very different. Write down FOUR ways in which slaves might have been taken for ordinary citizens. (In addition to the information you have read, the pictures on pp. 70–1 and 79 may give you ideas.)

2 Slaves varied very much in their value to a master, e.g. male or female, young or old, skilled or unskilled. Here is a list of some types of slave and, in the box below, some possible prices. Match up each type of slave with the price which you think would be appropriate.

Types of slave for sale

Male slave: Able to read and write.

Old female slave: Hardworking.

Young female: A pretty singer.

Young male: Big and strong.

Possible prices

800 sestertii	2400 sestertii
3700 sestertii	9500 sestertii

A **sestertius** was a Roman coin.

3 On the right is an imaginary form for advertising the sale of a slave. With the help of the information you have read, fill in the spaces with details of your own choice, e.g. how he/she was enslaved, how many previous owners etc.

Name:

Age:

Country:

Previous history:

Skills:

Price:

Now read pp. 80–1, which explain how slaves might become freedmen and freedwomen.

4 Why might a master decide to free a slave?

5 Can you think of any reasons why slaves might *not* want to be set free?

6 Why do you think people did not try to abolish slavery at this time?

The picture of the **manūmissiō** ceremony on p. 69 shows a magistrate holding the rod with which he has just freed two slaves. The standing one is shaking hands with his master (whose figure has been destroyed) while the other one kneels in gratitude. Note the pointed hats they are wearing. These were a sign that they were now freedmen.

Worksheet Master 6.5 is a game based on the lives of two slaves.

Check

Practising the language pp. 76–7

Ex. 1 Read the story **avārus** and work out the answers to the questions.

If you are in a group, this would be a good passage on which to work together.

Check

Ex. 2 This exercise revises the nominative plural forms which you met in Stage 5. Be careful to distinguish between these and the singular forms. You may need to refer back to Stage 5 pp. 59–60 and 62 before beginning the exercise. The exercise also practises the imperfect and perfect tenses.

Without writing a translation, work out the answers and meanings for sentences **a**, **c** and **e**. Then complete and write out sentences **b**, **d** and **f**, and translate them into English.

Check

Vocabulary checklist 6 p. 82

Learn the checklist.

1 Explain the connection between these pairs of words; one is in Latin, one in English.

| lībertus | *liberty* | cubiculum | *cubicle* | pulsat | *pulse* |
| scrībit | *scribe* | vēndit | *vendor* | | |

2 You might use the words *ferocious* and *furtive* to describe certain people. What other words could you use instead to mean the same?

3 Can you translate these short words?

| ōlim tum per quod tuus |

4 Translate these pairs of words.

| festīnat; festīnābat | vituperat; vituperāvērunt |
| superat; superāvit | abest; aberant |

5 These words have the same beginning as the Latin word **postquam**. What do they mean?

| postpone post-mortem postscript |

6 In the checklist **rēs** is given the meaning *thing*, but it can be translated in many other ways depending on the context. For example, at the end of the trial of Hermogenes in Stage 4, the judge says

ānulus rem probat.

*The ring proves the **case**.*

In this Stage you met the sentence

tum pater tōtam rem nārrāvit.

What would be a suitable meaning for **rem** here?

Check

Language test

1 Here are a number of words in different tenses. Tick those which are **imperfect**. Then sort out the rest into **present** and **perfect** and write them down in the appropriate section in the table.

ambulāvit	vidēbant	vocāvērunt	dormit
stant	petis	stābat	ambulant
petīvit	scrībit	dormiēbant	superās
videō	scrībēbat	vocat	superāvērunt

Present				
Perfect				

2 Complete the sentences by ticking the correct word, then translate the completed sentences. Be careful to translate the tenses correctly.

a vēnālīcius ancillam _____.
  (vēndēbat, vēndēbant)

b puer iānuam _____.
  (pulsāvit, pulsāvērunt)

c āctōrēs fābulam _____.
  (agit, agunt)

d māter puellam _____.
  (vituperat, vituperant)

e fūrēs ad forum _____.
  (vēnit, vēnērunt)

f multī mercātōrēs _____.
  (aderat, aderant)

 Check

Progress record

Stage 6 Fēlīx	Done	Revised	Any problems?
Model sentences			
pugna			
Fēlīx			
Fēlīx et fūr			
About the language			
Slaves and freedmen			
Practising the language			
Vocabulary checklist 6			
Language test			

Stage 7 cēna

In this Stage Caecilius gives two dinner-parties. In the first one, described in the model sentences, he entertains a friend, and they spend a pleasant evening together; the second party is larger and includes Felix among the guests.

At both parties the guests tell stories, a popular entertainment among the Romans. Felix tells a weird story, which is followed by the mysterious death of a missing guest.

Picture p. 83

Mosaic of a skeleton butler, holding a wine jug in each hand. It was found in a dining-room in Pompeii. Such images of death were quite common in dining-rooms and were meant to remind people that life was short and that they should enjoy themselves while they could.

Model sentences pp. 84–5

Study the sentences and work out the meaning. Here are the more difficult words.

pōculum	*wine-cup*	hausit	*drained*	plausit	*applauded*
surrēxērunt	*got up*	aperuērunt	*opened*	valē	*goodbye*

Check

If you have translated the second sentence in each pair correctly, go on to **fābula mīrābilis** on p. 86. If not, read **About the language**, paragraphs 1 and 2 on p. 87 and then see if you understand the **Model sentences**.

fābula mīrābilis p. 86

Read lines 1–7 and work out the meaning. Then answer these questions.

1 Who was at the dinner-party?

2 **coquum laudāvērunt** (line 2). What kind of thing would they have said to Grumio?

3 Who was expected, but didn't turn up?

4 What did Caecilius do about it?

Translate the story that Felix told (lines 8–16).

Check

Think of a newspaper headline that might have appeared over a report of this incident. If you like, you could write the newspaper report, too.

Look at the picture on p. 86. How has the artist tried to get the idea of a werewolf across to you? Could you do better? You might add your picture to your newspaper headline or report.

About the language 1 p. 87

If you have not already read them, read paragraphs 1 and 2 now. Read paragraph 3 and then translate the sentences in paragraph 4. (Pay special attention to sentence **d**.)

Check

Picture p. 87

Can you identify the scraps of food and suggest which courses at a **cēna** they belonged to? If necessary, see pp. 24–5.

Check

Decēns p. 88

The story so far   Decens had been invited to Caecilius' dinner-party, but had not turned up. Clemens had been sent to investigate. Meanwhile Felix had told the guests the story of the werewolf.

Now read the stage directions and the play as far as line 9, where two slaves come in.

These slaves had been escorting Decens to the party. They tell Caecilius the tragic story of their meeting with an armed gladiator.

Read lines 10–32 and write down the answers to the following questions:

1 Where did Decens meet the gladiator?

2 Why did the gladiator terrify Decens (lines 14–15)?

3 What did the gladiator think Decens was?

4 What did Decens think of the gladiator (line 19)?

5 Where did the gladiator drag Decens?

6 How did Clemens come to discover his body?

7 What was Caecilius' explanation of the death of Decens?

8 What other explanations might there be?

Check

About the language 2 p. 90

Read the notes. Then complete the English meanings in the pairs of words below.

mittit	s/he is sending, sends	mīsit	
īnspiciunt		īnspexērunt	they inspected
dēpōnit		dēposuit	s/he took off
plaudunt		plausērunt	

Check

post cēnam p. 89

Work out the meaning of the story and answer these questions.

1 Why were the friends so quiet as they made their way home?

2 What noise broke the silence?

3 What effect did it have on the friends?

4 Why were the Pompeians worried?

5 Why was Caecilius unaware of what was happening?

6 Here are some examples of the imperfect and perfect tenses taken from this story. Translate them and write **imperfect** or **perfect** by the side of each. The first one is done for you.

explicāvit	s/he explained	perfect
discessērunt		
ululāvit		
timēbant		
ruērunt		
dormiēbat		

Check

Roman beliefs about life after death pp. 93–5

Read this section and study the pictures and their captions. There is a further picture on p. 96.

1 How did people keep the memory of the dead alive in Roman times?

2 Why is the excavation of ancient tombs sometimes very helpful to archaeologists?

3 Look at the picture below.

    a What sort of procession is coming down the street?

    b Why might the man on the right be selling food in this particular place?

    c What is the group of three people closest to the procession doing? Why?

4 Here are four inscriptions from Roman tombstones. Read them and answer these questions.

   a What do each of the people who wrote them seem to believe about life after death?

   b What beliefs are there about life after death today?

Check

1

HERE TWIN BROTHERS ARE STRETCHED

SIDE BY SIDE IN THEIR TOMBS.

ON EARTH THEY WERE WELL MATCHED.

NOW EARTH BRINGS THEM TOGETHER AGAIN.

THEY WERE BORN BARBARIANS BUT

THEY WERE BORN AGAIN IN THE FOUNTAIN.

THEY GIVE THEIR SOULS TO HEAVEN AND THEIR

BODIES TO THE SOIL.

THEIR FATHER, FRAGILLA, AND HIS WIFE

FELT HEART-BROKEN AND WOULD MUCH RATHER

THAT THEY HAD DIED FIRST.

BUT THEY CAN BEAR THEIR SADNESS,

FOR CHRIST IS GENTLE.

THEY HAVE NOT LOST THEIR CHILDREN.

THEY HAVE GIVEN THEM AS A PRESENT TO GOD.

2

DO NOT IGNORE MY EPITAPH, PASSER-BY,

BUT LINGER A WHILE.

DO NOT POUR OFFERINGS OF WINE OVER MY GRAVE;

DO NOT DECORATE IT WITH GARLANDS - IT IS ONLY

A STONE. DON'T LIGHT A FIRE ON MY BEHALF - IT'S

ALL A WASTE OF MONEY!

IF YOU HAVE ANYTHING TO GIVE SHARE IT WITH

SOMEONE WHO IS ALIVE. IF YOU POUR WINE ON MY

ASHES YOU WILL ONLY BE MAKING A MUDDY MESS -

THE DEAD WILL NOT DRINK IT. THIS IS WHAT WILL

BECOME OF ME, SO WHEN YOU SCATTER EARTH ON

MY REMAINS SAY, 'THIS WAS A MAN BUT NOW IT IS

NOTHING: IT HAS RETURNED TO WHAT IT WAS.'

COMMIT NO WILFUL DAMAGE TO THIS

TOMB

3

TO THE GHOSTS OF THE DEAD

I, C. TULLIUS HESPER, HAVE MADE THIS

ALTAR FOR MY BONES. IF ANYBODY DISTURBS THEM

OR THROWS THEM OUT THEN I HOPE THAT HE LIVES

FOR A LONG TIME IN PAIN, AND THAT WHEN HE IS

DEAD, THE DEAD WILL NOT ALLOW HIM INTO THE

UNDERWORLD.

4

I·WAS·A·YOVNG·GIRL·
AND·MY·FAMILY·LOVED·ME·
HERE·I·AM·DEAD◄ I·AM·ASH
AND·THE·ASH·IS·EARTH ◄ BVT·F·
EARTH·IS·A·GODDESS·THEN·
I·AM·A·GODDESS·TOO
AND
I·AM·NOT·DEAD
STRANGER·PLEASE·DON'T·
DISTVRB·MY·BONES·
MVS
AGED· XIII ·

Practising the language p. 92

Ex. 1 Read the example. Why is **cēnam laudāvērunt** the correct choice? If you need a clue, think whether **amīcī** is singular or plural. Now work through the examples as instructed. Be extra careful with **g**.

Ex. 2 This exercise will show whether you know the difference between nominative and accusative cases and singular and plural. If you have problems with **a**, **b**, **e**, **g** or **h**, read p. 21 again; with **c**, **d**, **f**, **i** or **j**, read p. 62 again.

 Check

Metella et Melissa p. 91

This story provides a change of mood after the ghost story. Read it and then answer these questions.

1 Why did Metella go into the kitchen?

2 How did Grumio show that he was angry (line 3)?

3 Where did Metella go next?

4 'Melissa est pestis!' Explain why Clemens was angry (lines 10–14).

5 Where was Melissa?

6 'Melissa, cūr lacrimās?' What answer did Melissa give (lines 18–19)?

7 Read the last paragraph. Give two ways in which Melissa looks after Metella.

8 How has Metella's attitude to Melissa changed since she came to work in the villa?

 Check

Vocabulary checklist 7 p. 96

Learn the checklist.

1 *The Rime of the Ancient Mariner* is a **narrative** poem. What does that mean?

2 An **intelligent** person is one who

a knows a lot;

b understands things;

c has a good memory.

Which is the most accurate description?

3 Why are the gods called **immortals**?

4 Why is a **factory** so called?

5 Sports reporters sometimes tell us that one of the teams in a match was **annihilated**, but what does this really mean?

6 A carnivorous animal eats flesh; a herbivorous one eats grass: what does an animal eat if it is **omnivorous**?

7 What would you expect an **interrogator** to do?

8 If you have a **tacit** agreement with someone, what kind of agreement is it?

 Check

Language test

1 Translate these sentences:

   a Clēmēns fortis erat. amphitheātrum intrāvit.

   b amīcī per urbem ruērunt. umbram timēbant.

   c lībertus fūrem petīvit. īnfantem servāvit.

   d mercātor erat īrātus. agricolam vituperābat.

   e Pompēiānī in theātrō sedēbant. magnum clāmōrem faciēbant.

2 Read this story. Make a list of the words in **bold type** and say what tense (perfect, imperfect or present) you would use if you had to translate them into Latin.

A philosopher called Cleodemus was very ill with a fever. He **was lying** awake in bed, when a handsome young man in a white cloak **appeared** by his bed. He **helped** Cleodemus to get up and then **led** him down through a cave into the Underworld. They **came** to a hall where Pluto, the King of the Underworld, **was reading** a book in which were written the names of those who were about to die. When the King **saw** Cleodemus, he was angry with the young man and **said**, 'This man is not on my list. Take him back to earth and bring me the blacksmith, Demylus, who **lives** next to this man.'

    While Cleodemus **was returning** to earth the fever **left** him and he felt well again. When he **reached** his house he **met** a band of mourners. 'Alas!' they said, 'Your neighbour Demylus **is dying**.'

3 Translate these perfect and imperfect tenses:

a	cēnāvit	f	discessit
b	lacrimāvērunt	g	dīxērunt
c	cōnspexit	h	nārrābat
d	rogābat	i	plausērunt
e	terrēbant	j	fēcit

4 In the table below, only TWO of the Latin sentences are correct. Tick the sentences which are correct and write down ONE incorrect word from each of the other three sentences.

Latin sentence	Tick	Incorrect word
a coquus in culīnā labōrāvērunt.		
b amīcī in triclīniō bibēbant.		
c dominus erant in forō.		
d fēminae in tabernā stābat.		
e māter erat in ātriō.		

Check

Progress record   Textbook pp. 83–96   Student Study Book pp. 36–41

Stage 7 cēna	Done	Revised	Any problems?
Model sentences			
fābula mīrābilis			
About the language 1			
Decēns			
About the language 2			
post cēnam			
Roman beliefs about life after death			
Practising the language			
Metella et Melissa			
Vocabulary checklist 7			
Language test			

Stage 8 gladiātōrēs

One of the most popular entertainments in the Roman world was the gladiatorial show in which armed men fought one another – often to the death. The shows took place in a building called an amphitheatre like the one in Pompeii shown in this picture. How is the amphitheatre different from the theatre? How is it similar? Look back at p. 56 if necessary.

Check

Picture p. 97

Top surface of a clay lamp, showing two fighters. They are armed with helmets, greaves (leg shields), protection on their sword arms, straight swords and oblong shields. One of the fighters has dropped his shield.

Model sentences pp. 98–9

The sentences start with the announcement in the forum of a show at Pompeii and end with the fighting in the amphitheatre.

Study the sentences and work out the meaning. Here are the more difficult new words.

nūntiābant	*were announcing*
clausae	*closed*
murmillōnēs	*murmillones, gladiators of a special type*
saepe	*often*

Now answer the following questions:

p. 98 **Sentences 1** Who were listening to the messengers?

Sentences 2 Whom were the Pompeians praising?

Sentence 3 Whom did the girls greet?

p. 99 **Sentence 4** Whom were the slaves looking at?

Sentence 6 What did the Pompeians *not* do?

Sentence 9 Whom were the spectators urging on?

Check

You will have noticed that the pictures on p. 97 and pp. 98–9 show different types of gladiator. Find out about them and the shows by reading **Gladiatorial shows** at the end of the Stage.

Gladiatorial shows pp. 107–10

When you have read this section and studied the pictures answer the following questions.

1 Why do you think the shows were so popular?

2 Are there any similar modern entertainments?

3 Here are translations of three graffiti about gladiators that were scribbled on walls at Pompeii.

a All the best to Fabius the Thracian!

b Crescens the retiarius, who can do what he likes with the girls.

c A beast fight will be held here on 28th August and Felix will fight the bears.

Match the graffiti above with the pictures below. Write the appropriate letters in the boxes beside the pictures.

Check

gladiātōrēs p. 100

Read the first paragraph aloud and work out the meaning in your head. Write out a translation of the second and third paragraphs.

Complete this translation of the last paragraph.

After the Pompeians heard the _____, they _____ to the amphitheatre as quickly as possible. The Nucerians _____ hurried to the amphitheatre. All _____ loudly. After the Pompeians and the Nucerians _____ _____ , they fell silent. _____ were waiting for

_____ .

Check

in arēnā p. 101

In your head, translate the cartoon version of the story on page 45 of this book, using the vocabulary on p. 101. You may then like to translate the whole story.

1

duo rētiāriī

rētiāriī Nūcerīnōs valdē dēlectābant.

duo murmillōnēs

murmillōnēs Pompēiānōs valdē dēlectābant.

2

Pompēiānī spectātōrēs

Nucerīnī spectātōrēs

murmillōnēs rētiāriōs frūstrā ad pugnam prōvocāvērunt.

3

murmillō et rētiāriī ferōciter pugnāvērunt.

rētiāriī tandem murmillōnem graviter vulnerāvērunt.

4 tum rētiāriī alterum murmillōnem petīvērunt.

hic murmillō fortiter pugnābat, sed rētiāriī eum quoque superāvērunt.

5

Pompēiānī missiōnem postulābant, quod murmillōnēs fortēs erant.

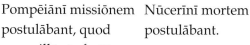

omnēs tacēbant et Rēgulum intentē spectābant.

Nūcerīnī mortem postulābant.

Rēgulus, quod Nūcerīnī mortem postulābant, pollicem vertit.

6 Pompēiānī erant īrātī et vehementer clāmābant.

rētiāriī tamen, postquam Rēgulus signum dedit, murmillōnēs interfēcērunt.

Check

About the language 1 p. 102

Read paragraphs 1, 2 and 3. Learn the nominative and accusative forms in paragraph 3. Translate paragraph 4.

Further exercise Here is a list of words. Put a tick in the box that gives the correct description of the words. In two cases you can tick two boxes.

	nominative singular	accusative singular	nominative plural	accusative plural
ancillam				
nūntiōs				
viās				
spectātōrēs				
mortem				
bēstiās				
rētiāriī				
gladiātōrēs				
pugna				
puerum				

Check

vēnātiō p. 103

1 Work out the meaning and answer the questions.

2 Read the first paragraph again and write out two sentences containing an accusative plural. Underline the accusative plural and translate the sentences.

3 The story you have just read is made up, but we know that the people of Pompeii and Nuceria actually did fight each other on one occasion. Read Tacitus' account of the riot on p. 111 and study the drawing of the wall-painting found in Pompeii. Part of the actual wall-painting appears on p. 107.

   What disturbances happen at sporting events today? How similar are they to the riot portrayed in Tacitus' report and in the pictures?

   Check

pāstor et leō p. 104

This is a famous story and a good one to act. First work out the meaning. Then allot the parts. You will need a shepherd, a lion and one or two narrators. (Narrator 1 could read the Latin in lines 1–14, narrator 2 the rest of the story.)

Check

About the language 2 p. 105

Read paragraph 1 and translate the sentences in paragraph 2.

Further exercise When you have done this see if you can think what the following superlatives might be and write them below. Fill in the other gaps too. The first example is done for you.

		Superlative	
doctus	skilful	doctissimus	very skilful
ignāvus	cowardly		very cowardly
obscūrus	dark		very dark
occupātus	busy		
pretiōsus			very precious

Check

Practising the language p. 106

Ex. 1 First write out the meanings of the six words in the box on the right of the exercise. Then fill in the gaps in the sentences with the correct Latin word and translate.

Ex. 2 Write out this exercise.

Check

Vocabulary checklist 8 p. 112

Learn the checklist.

1 What is the origin of the title of *Duke*, as in 'The Duke of Edinburgh'?

2 Why are *gladiators* so called?

3 What part of your body do you use to propel a *pedalo*?

4 'Don't be so *puerile*.' What are you being accused of?

5 What does a *pugnacious* person like doing?

6 The word *spectacles* can have two different meanings. What are they? How are they related to **spectāculum**?

Check

Language test

1   Read the sentences and tick the Latin word which correctly translates the word in **bold type**.

  a The girl lost the **ring**.

  (ānulum, ānulōs)

  b The miser had no **friends**.

  (amīcum, amīcōs)

  c The young men knocked on the **door**.
  (iānuam, iānuās)

  d The slave had very big **feet**.

  (pedem, pedēs)

  e The merchant has lost all his **ships**.

  (nāvem, nāvēs)

2   Translate these sentences. Then write down the case of the word in **bold type** and say whether it is singular or plural, for example:

  Pompēiānī **nūntiōs** salūtāvērunt.

  The Pompeians greeted the messengers. (accusative plural)

  a **pāstor** silvam intrāvit.

  b murmillōnēs **gladiōs** quaesīvērunt.

  c servī **portam** aperuērunt.

  d **cīvēs** mortem postulāvērunt.

  e spectātōrēs **leōnēs** incitāvērunt.

3   Translate these sentences:

  a canēs ferōcissimī lupum superāvērunt.

  b puellae mātrem nōtissimam habēbant.

  c Pompēiānī gladiātōrēs fortissimōs laudāvērunt.

  d leō erat laetissimus quod pēs nōn dolēbat.

  e hospitēs, postquam cēnāvērunt, fābulam longissimam audīvērunt.

 Check

Revision

1   You have now met all the verb tenses for Book I. Turn to p. 189 and read paragraphs 4 and 5. Then work out the meanings of the words in paragraph 6 on p. 190. You will need to look up the last word **accēpit** in the **Vocabulary**.

2   Read paragraph 7. Then translate these two further examples.

  pater in forō negōtium agēbat.

  āctōrēs in theātrō fābulam agēbant.

Check

Progress record Textbook pp. 97–112 Student Study Book pp. 43–8

Stage 8 gladiātōrēs	Done	Revised	Any problems?
Model sentences			
Gladiatorial shows			
gladiātōrēs			
in arēnā			
About the language 1			
vēnātiō			
pāstor et leō			
About the language 2			
Practising the language			
Vocabulary checklist 8			
Language test			
Revision			

Stage 9 thermae

The Pompeians enjoyed their entertainments and leisure time. You have already read about their dinner-parties as well as the plays in the theatre and gladiatorial shows in the amphitheatre. They also enjoyed their daily visit to the public baths. In AD 79 there were three sets of **thermae** and a fourth, the Central Baths, was being built.

Look at the plan of Pompeii in Stage 3, p. 34 and note the site of each of these **thermae**.

Picture p. 113

The centre of the entrance hall in a set of baths in Herculaneum. A jet of water came from the bust of the god Apollo and fell into the basin in front.

Model sentences pp. 114–15

Study the sentences. Work out the meaning and answer the questions. Here are some new words.

novum	new	ferēbat	was carrying	ēmīsit	sent out, threw
percussit	hit, struck	dōnum	gift, present	ēlēgit	chose

Sentence 2	What did Quintus do with his money at the baths?
Sentences 4	What did he do with his discus when he met his friends?
Sentences 7	Why was Metella walking in the forum?
Sentences 8	What did the merchant do?
Sentences 9	What happened after Metella chose a toga?
Sentences 10	Why was Grumio in the kitchen?
Sentences 12	When did the slave-girl begin to sing? *Check*

The baths pp. 124–7

Read to the end of the first paragraph on p. 124 and study the pictures. You will follow Caecilius and his friends as they visit the different areas in the baths. In the table below, write down the English meaning of each area and describe what people did in them.

Latin name	English	Activities
palaestra		
apodytērium		
tepidārium		
caldārium		
frigidārium		

Check

in palaestrā pp. 116–17

Read the story in sections as follows:

Lines 1–9 Work out the meaning in your head and then answer questions 1–4.

Lines 10–16 Write out a translation and answer question 5.

Lines 17–33 Work out the meaning in your head. Answer questions 6–10. Before answering the second part of question 10 you may find it helpful to re-read the story from line 15 to the end. If you are in a group, you could compare your answers.

Check

The baths continued pp. 124–7

Revise what you have read so far in this section and then read to the end.

You will see from the plan of the Forum Baths on p. 127 that there were separate baths for women. In some towns, where these did not exist, the women would use the baths in the morning and the men would use them in the afternoon.

Answer these questions. If you are in a group, half of you could do question 3 and half of you question 5 and then compare answers.

1   Suggest English words connected with **thermae**, **tepidārium** and **frigidārium**. What is the connection?

2   Many different people worked in the baths to cater for the needs of the bathers. Make a list of those mentioned in the text. Are there others that must have been there, but are not mentioned?

3   This section mentions several materials or products connected with the baths or the objects used there. Explain what each product in the list was used for and where you would find it: brick, metal, stone, lead, marble, wood.

4   What are the objects in this picture? What were they used for?

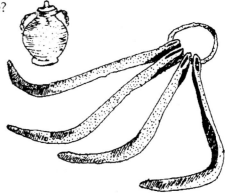

5   If an ancient Pompeian were living in modern Britain, where would he go to enjoy the equivalent leisure activities? What differences would he find? Do people today have the same reasons for visiting the public baths?

Check

Worksheet Master 9.5 is a picture exercise on the baths and the activities that took place in them.

About the language pp. 118–19

Read paragraphs 1–3. When you look at the cases of the noun in paragraph 3, you will see that the form **puellae** can also be the nominative plural. You may feel worried about confusing these cases but it is really not a big problem when you have the meaning of the story to help you.

Now translate the sentences in paragraph 4.

Further exercises   **1**   Look back at the **Model sentences** on pp. 114–15; write out and translate FOUR sentences containing a dative case. Underline the Latin words that are dative.

2   Read paragraph 5 on p. 119. In the English passage below write down in the brackets the correct Latin forms for the words in **bold type**.

> **You** (   ) are my friend. **I** (   ) see **you** (   ) every day. **I** (   ) enjoy work but **you** (   ) are unhappy when the master gives a job **to you** (   ). **You** (   ) ask **me** (   ) to help **you** (   ) and promise to give a reward **to me** (   ).

Check

in tabernā p. 120

Read lines 1–18 and answer these questions.

1   Which THREE kinds of clothing were being sold in the shop?

2   Give a complete list of the people in the shop, both individuals and groups.

Read lines 19–35.

3   The kind of buying and selling described here is called bargaining and still takes place in many countries today. To show how the bargaining proceeded, fill in the two columns, one giving Marcellus' prices, the other the women's offers.

Marcellus' prices	Women's offers

4   Who makes the final decision?

5   What was Melissa's part in the story?

6   How did the merchant behave? What does his behaviour tell you about his character?

Check

Worksheet Master 9.4 is a play based on this story.

Practising the language p. 121

Exs. 1 and 2 These two exercises are rather challenging. Before attempting them, you will find it helpful to re-read paragraphs 1–3 on pp. 118–19. Make sure that you can recognise both the singular and plural forms of the nominative and accusative. Then examine again carefully the forms of the dative.

When you have done this, write out a translation of the sentences in Exercise 1.
Check

If all your answers are correct, work through Exercise 2 without writing it out. If you have made a number of mistakes in Exercise 1, write out Exercise 2 also for further practice.

Ex. 3 You need not write out this exercise. If you are in a group, you could work through it together orally.
Check

in apodytēriō p. 122

Read the play, work out the meaning and answer these questions.

1 Where are Sceledrus and Anthrax at the beginning of the story? What job are they doing?

2 Which of the two slaves seems to be the more reliable? Give a reason for your choice.

3 What is the thief doing when he is observed (lines 12–13)?

4 'ēheu!' (line 19). Why does the merchant say this?

5 How is the thief treated at the end of the story?

6 Sceledrus and Anthrax are slaves. How can you tell from the story that the thief is a free man? Who do you think had the more comfortable life?

7 In lines 2–11 the words **ego** and **tū** have generally been omitted because the endings of the verbs show which person is doing the action. For example, in line 2, **labōrās = tū labōrās**. Pick out the other verbs and put with them the missing **ego** or **tū**.

8 Look at the mosaics on pp. 122 and 128 and read the captions. What is a *marine theme*? Why is it suitable for the baths?

If you are in a group, you may like to act the play in Latin or in English.
Check

Vocabulary checklist 9 p. 128

Learn the checklist. Below is a table with some of the Latin words in the checklist, and a pool of English words. Next to each Latin word write down the English word which is connected with it, and explain the connection.

Latin	English	Connection
hospes		
iterum		
prōcēdit		
īnspicit		
medius		
celeriter		
trādit		
homō		

medium	inspection	homicide	procedure
accelerate	hospitality	reiterate	tradition

Check

Language test

1 Tick the correct form in the brackets for the words in **bold type**.

    a The slave was offering a wine cup **to the guest**. (hospitī, hospitibus)

    b The girls showed the dog **to the slaves**. (servō, servīs)

    c The shopkeeper sold the ring **to the woman**. (fēminae, fēminīs)

    d You gave the sword **to me**. (mē, mihi)

    e The citizens handed over **the thief** to the judge. (fūrem, fūrī)

    f The master bought **the dresses** for his wife. (stolās, stolīs)

2 Translate these sentences.

    a coquus cēnam dominō parābat.

    b homō togam mercātōrī vēndidit.

    c servī multās tunicās iuvenibus ostendērunt.

    d cūr tū mihi pecūniam dās?

    e puer athlētae discum trādidit.

Check

Revision

You have now met all the noun cases for Book I. Turn to p. 189 which explains how nouns are listed in the **Vocabulary**. Read paragraphs 1 and 2. Then find the nominative singular of the words in paragraph 3. Give the meaning of the words. All the answers can be found in the **Vocabulary**.

Progress record Textbook pp. 113–28 Student Study Book pp. 50–4

Stage 9 thermae	Done	Revised	Any problems?
Model sentences			
The baths			
in palaestrā			
The baths continued			
About the language			
in tabernā			
Practising the language			
in apodytēriō			
Vocabulary checklist 9			
Language test			
Revision			

Stage 10 rhētor

In this Stage you will read about the education given to young Pompeians. Look at the picture in which a schoolmaster is teaching a group of pupils. Then answer these questions.

1   Name THREE items which would be in your class but which are not in the picture.
2   Where do you think the lesson is taking place?

Check

Picture p. 129

A marble statue of an elderly Greek teaching. Look at his hand and suggest what he might be saying to his class of Pompeian boys. *Check*

Model sentences pp. 130–3

pp. 130–1   Study the sentences and work out the meaning. Then answer these questions. Here are some of the new words.

| pontēs | *bridges* | aedificāmus | *build* | fundōs | *farms* |

1   What special skills does the Roman claim to have?
2   Translate what the Greek says in reply.
3   What is the meaning of the Latin word **nōs**?
4   What do you think is the purpose of the instruments in the pictures at the top of pp. 130–1?

If you are in a group, it would be useful to compare your answers at this point. *Check*

pp. 132–3   Study the sentences and work out the meaning. Then answer the questions.

| ūtilēs | *useful* | docēmus | *teach* |

5   To whom does the Roman refer when he uses the word **vōs**? To whom does the Greek refer when he uses the same word?
6   Look at the picture at the top of p. 133. Who do you think the men are and what are they doing?
7   Who makes the final point – the Roman or the Greek? Do you think it is a convincing statement to make?
8   Which of these words would best describe the conversation between the Roman and the Greek: discussion, debate, argument?
9   In what way are the various skills of the Romans similar to each other? In what way are the various skills of the Greeks similar to each other?

Check

controversia pp. 134–5

Read lines 1–13 and find out what is happening in the first part of the story. Test your understanding by choosing from the pool of English words the correct one to complete each of the sentences.

| debate | colonnade | opinion | Greek | proof | Romans | sports ground |

1 Quintus and Alexander were on their way to the _____ .

2 The teacher held his classes in the _____ at the sports ground.

3 Alexander and Theodorus were both _____ .

4 The lesson for the day was in the form of a _____ .

5 Quintus thought that _____ were better than Greeks.

6 Theodorus did not accept this _____ .

7 Quintus had to put forward his _____ .

Check

Read lines 14–22. Quintus, in his speech, makes several statements which he follows up with his proof. His statements are listed in the table below. Choose THREE of them. Write down the proof that Quintus gives in the space provided and say whether you think his statements and proofs are strong or weak. Give a reason. This would be a good group activity.

Quintus' statement	Quintus' proof	Your comments
1 We Romans are very brave.		
2 We keep the peace.		
3 We are excellent architects.		
4 We Romans work hard.		
5 You Greeks are lazy.		

Now write out an English translation of lines 23–34.

Do you agree or disagree with Theodorus' decision and his reason for it? (Support your answer by referring to the story.) Could he have had another reason for this decision?

Check

Schools pp. 140–3

Read the information and then answer the questions. If you are in a group, you could divide up the questions and then discuss your answers.

1 In the story **contrōversia** on pp. 134–5 at which stage of his education would Quintus be? Which subjects would he already have learned and which would he be studying at the time of the story?

2 Why would a girl not be studying in the school of the **grammaticus**?

3 Look at the first picture on p. 142.

    a What would the boys have used to write with on the papyrus rolls?

    b What other kind of writing material is shown in the picture?

    c Who do you think the person standing up on the right might be?

4 Suppose you were a boy of fifteen in Pompeii about to leave school. What would be your next step if you were going to be (a) a lawyer, or (b) an architect?

5 In reading about schools, you have met several Latin words from which English words have been derived, though the meaning may sometimes have been changed.

    a **lūdī magister** means schoolteacher or school _____ .

    b **paedagōgus:** Look up in an English dictionary the word *pedagogue*. What does it mean? How has the meaning changed from that of **paedagōgus**?

    c **grammaticus, rhētor:** These words give us two English words connected with language. What are they? Use your dictionary again, if necessary.

Check

About the language 1 p. 136

Read paragraphs 1–3 and observe carefully the new verb endings. Then, without writing them out, work out the meaning of the sentences in paragraph 4; take special care when doing sentences **c** and **d**.

Check

Further exercise Read paragraph 5; then fill in the blank spaces in these sentences by adding one of the words: **ego, tū, nōs, vōs**; or one of the verb endings: **-ō, -s, -mus, -tis**. Translate the completed sentences.

1 _____ sedēmus.

2 tū venī_____.

3 _____ spectātis.

4 ego intr_____.

5 nōs contendi_____.

6 _____ labōrās.

7 _____ sum callidus.

8 vōs es_____ frātrēs.

Check

statuae p. 137

Read lines 1–28 and work out in your head what happens in the story up to this point. Then write down evidence from the story to prove the truth of these statements.

If you are working in a group, it would be useful to discuss your answers when you have each worked out your own evidence.

1　Quintus was not upset that Alexander had beaten him in the debate.

2　Alexander had twin brothers.

3　Alexander was not very sensible when he bought the statues.

4　Alexander's brothers were greedy and selfish.

5　Alexander was often angry with his brothers' behaviour.

6　Thrasymachus had a worse temper than Diodorus.

Now write out an English translation of lines 29–37.

Further questions

1　At the end of the story, how does Quintus prove the point he was making in the debate? (Refer back to **contrōversia** lines 15–17.)

2　What do you think Thrasymachus meant by his last remark? Why did he whisper it?

3　Look at the statuettes at the bottom of p. 137. Identify them and say who received each of them.

Check

About the language 2 p. 138

Read paragraph 1 and write out the further examples in paragraph 2. Read paragraph 3.

What does **quam** mean in all these sentences?

Further exercise　Choosing suitable words from the pool, make up THREE sentences similar to the ones in paragraphs 1 and 2, comparing people or things. Then translate your sentences into English.

For example:

canis est ferōcior quam leō.

The dog is fiercer than the lion.

montēs erant pulchriōrēs quam urbēs.

The mountains were more beautiful than the cities.

Remember to use:

singular nouns with singular verbs and
　　comparatives

plural nouns with plural verbs and
　　comparatives.

Check

People or things	
amīcus	āctōrēs
canis	gladiātōrēs
frāter	dominae
servus	urbēs
leō	ancillae
lībertus	montēs

Comparatives	
laetior	pulchriōrēs
callidior	maiōrēs
ferōcior	nōtiōrēs

Verbs	
est	sunt
erat	erant

ānulus Aegyptius pp. 138–9

Read the story and answer the questions. Give all the necessary detail, especially for questions 5, 6 and 8, which require longer answers.

Check

What do you think happened after the end of this story? If you have time, write a sequel. (If you are in a group, you could each make up a story and then read it out.)

Picture p. 139

This bronze ring is decorated with heads of two Egyptian deities: the goddess Isis on the left and the god Serapis on the right.

Practising the language p. 140

Both these exercises are testing vocabulary and comprehension but at the same time they are giving further practice with **nōs** and **vōs**. You should not find it difficult to understand the sentences and there is no need to write them out. If you are in a group, you could read each sentence in turn first in Latin and then in English.

Check

Vocabulary checklist 10 p. 144

Learn the checklist.

1 The French revolutionaries proclaimed 'Liberty, Equality and *Fraternity*'. What is *fraternity*?

2 Why was the *Pacific* Ocean so named?

3 What is an *inhabitant* of a place? What is the natural *habitat* of a plant or animal?

4 We are often asked to *conserve* water and *preserve* the natural environment. From which Latin word are the two English ones derived?

5 Is a *taciturn* person likely to utter *exclamations*? Give a reason for your answer.

6 In the word square you will find ELEVEN Latin words from the checklist. The words are written in a straight line but may be forward, backwards, up, down or diagonal. Write down the words with their English meanings.

V	R	I	U	M	R	N	E	P	S
E	T	A	I	T	N	U	N	U	T
H	B	R	O	X	U	C	T	A	S
E	I	A	C	C	P	R	V	A	R
M	L	L	P	V	O	R	P	E	E
E	S	E	M	P	E	R	U	A	B
N	N	I	A	S	O	L	U	S	I
T	E	X	A	I	N	E	V	L	L
E	C	A	L	L	I	D	U	S	A
R	M	U	I	R	E	P	M	I	A

Latin word   **Meaning**

1 _____   _____

2 _____   _____

3 _____   _____

4 _____   _____

5 _____   _____

6 _____   _____

7 _____   _____

8 _____   _____

9 _____   _____

10 _____   _____

11 _____   _____

Check

Language test

1 From the box choose the appropriate word for each space in the passage below. Then write out a translation of the passage.

habēmus	semper	stultiōrēs
habētis	vōs	quam
turbulentior	īmus	sumus

nōs Pompēiānī sumus callidissimī. nōs maximum amphitheātrum _____ .

spectāculum saepe in amphitheātrō spectāmus. vōs Nūcerīnī estis _____

quam Pompēiānī. vōs amphitheātrum nōn _____ . vōs _____

ad amphitheātrum Pompēiānum venītis.

nōs Pompēiānī _____ contentī. nōs cotīdiē ad thermās _____ .

thermae Pompēiānōs dēlectant.

Nūceria est urbs _____ quam Pompēiī. _____ Nūcerīnī

semper pugnātis. vōs pācem nōn servātis.

vōs Nūcerīnī estis miserandī. nōs Pompēiānī sumus meliōrēs _____

vōs.

2 Complete the sentences by ticking the correct word in brackets. Then translate the completed sentences.

a nōs sumus pictōrēs; nōs pictūrās pulchrās _____ .

(pingimus, pingitis, pingunt)

b cīvēs sunt laetī; ad thermās _____ .

(venīmus, venītis, veniunt)

c ego sum callidus; pecūniam meam _____ .

(servō, servās, servat)

d rhētor est Graecus; contrōversiam _____ .

(nūntiō, nūntiās, nūntiat)

e Syphāx est vēnālīcius; tū _____ mercātor.

(sum, es, est)

Check

Revision

Nouns

Turn to p.180. Study paragraphs 1 and 2 and then do the exercise in paragraph 3.

Check

Learn the nouns in the table in paragraph 1. Then see if you can do the exercise in paragraph 4 without looking at the table.

Check

Progress record   Textbook pp. 129–44   Student Study Book pp. 56–62

Stage 10 rhētor	Done	Revised	Any problems?
Model sentences			
contrōversia			
Schools			
About the language 1			
statuae			
About the language 2			
ānulus Aegyptius			
Practising the language			
Vocabulary checklist 10			
Language test			
Revision			

Stage 11 candidātī

Elections were held every year in Pompeii to elect the officials. Their job was to look after law and order in the town and to see that local services were well run. In this drawing one of the candidates is shown making a speech to the voters.

Picture p. 145

This marble statue was erected in Pompeii in honour of Marcus Holconius Rufus, one of its most famous citizens. He and other members of his family, like the Holconius you will read about in this Stage, were regularly elected to the most important posts in the town.

Local government and elections pp. 156–9

Read pp. 156–7. Then look at the drawing above and answer the following questions:

1 Where in the forum is the candidate making his speech? If you need help, see p. 50.

2 What is the candidate wearing? What colour would it be?

3 It is likely that the candidate's name is Rufus, as this appears on the placard in the picture. Can you work out from the slogan on the placard who his supporters are and what office he is standing for?

4 Why could only wealthy men afford to stand for election?

5 What satisfaction might they expect if they were elected?

Check

Pictures p. 156

Top The officials who were presiding over the council sat at the far end of the hall. The recesses in the walls probably had statues in them and the brickwork would have been hidden beneath a marble facing.

Bottom You will see more clearly what is going on in this picture if you use the line drawing on the right to help you. Note that the circular loaves are similar to the one shown on p. 24 of your textbook.

Model sentences pp. 146–7

The first picture shows groups of Pompeians crowding round their candidates. The other pictures are portraits of the candidates and the sentences say what their supporters think of them.

Study the sentences and then translate them. If you are working in a group, you may each like to adopt one of the candidates and then read out your sentences to each other in English and Latin. You will need to know the following words:

noster	*our*
favēmus	*we favour, give support to*
crēdimus	*we trust, have faith in*

Check

Marcus et Quārtus p. 148

This and the next story are about two brothers, Marcus and Quartus, who support different candidates. Read lines 1–7, work out the meaning in your head and complete these sentences.

1 Marcus thinks _____ is the best candidate because _____ _____ . The Pompeians support him because _____ .

2 Quartus thinks _____ is the best candidate because _____ _____ . The Pompeians trust him because _____ .

Check

Write out a translation of lines 8–15.

Then work out the meaning of the rest of the story in your head and answer the following questions.

1 What job did Quartus give Sulla?

2 Why was it likely to annoy Marcus?

3 How much did Quartus pay Sulla?

4 Which Latin words show that Sulla actually carried out the work?

Check

Local government and elections continued pp. 158–9

Read **Election notices** on pp. 158–9 and study the pictures. There is a further picture on p. 160. You will find the slogans in the pictures difficult to understand because the sign-writers used abbreviations to save time and space. However, can you spot the abbreviations for duovir and aedile and the name of a candidate who is familiar to you from the stories? (All the inscriptions are printed out in full and translated in the *Answer Key*.)

Worksheet Master 11.3 has a collection of graffiti of various kinds. Most of them are like the ones found on walls today.

Check

About the language 1 p. 150

This note tells you more about the dative case. Note in particular the simpler and more usual meanings of **favet** and **crēdit** in paragraph 3.

Translate the further examples in paragraph 4.

Read paragraphs 5 and 6. Learn the new forms **nōbīs** and **vōbīs**, and revise **mihi** and **tibi**.

Further exercise Turn back to **Marcus et Quārtus** on p. 148. In lines 16–23 find SIX different words in the dative case and write them down.

Check

Sulla p. 149

This story is the sequel to **Marcus et Quārtus**. The sign-writer Sulla has just written up a slogan saying that Marcus and Quartus support Holconius. Read the following translation of lines 1–12, alongside the Latin.

Marcus came out of the house. He saw Sulla. He caught sight of the slogan. After he read the slogan, he was angry. Marcus cursed the sign-writer vehemently.

'Your brother invited me to the house', said Sulla. 'Your brother gave me ten denarii.'

'My brother is sillier than an ass', Marcus replied to Sulla. 'In our house I am the master, because I am the elder. Sulla, rub out that writing! Write a new slogan!'

Marcus gave Sulla fifteen denarii.

'Is that all right for you?' he asked.

'It's all right for me', Sulla replied to Marcus. After Sulla had rubbed out the writing, he wrote this slogan, 'Marcus and his brother support Afer. Marcus and his brother trust Afer.'

Now write out a translation of lines 13–18.

Check

Work out the meaning of the rest of the story in your head and answer the following questions:

1 **duōs titulōs ... scrīpsit** (line 21). What did these slogans say?

2 How would you describe the feelings of the brothers when they read the slogans?

3 **Sulla rīdēbat** (line 28). Why was Sulla doing this?

4 How much money did Sulla receive altogether from the brothers? (You will need to look at the previous story as well.)

5 Sulla calls the brothers **līberālissimī**. How would *you* describe them (in Latin or English)? Give a reason for your answer.

Check

About the language 2 p. 154

Read paragraph 1 and then work out the meaning of the further examples in paragraph 2. Write down a translation for examples **c**, **d**, **g** and **i**.

Check

Lūcius Spurius Pompōniānus pp. 151–3

This is a play with four scenes. If you are in a group, the play can be acted in Latin and English. To produce an English translation quickly, divide the group into two or four smaller groups and share out the scenes between the groups. Each group then reads out the translation of its scene so that everyone knows what the Latin means and has a good idea of the plot.

Answer the following questions about your scene. Some of the answers will help you with acting the play.

If you are on your own, translate each scene in your head. As you complete each scene, answer the questions that belong to it and check your answers.

in vīllā p. 151

1 Why does Clemens think Grumio ought to support Holconius?

2 Why does Grumio in fact support Afer?

3 When Grumio calls himself Lucius Spurius Pomponianus why does he give himself three names?

4 Why does Clemens describe Grumio's scheme as **perīculōsam** (line 22)?

prope amphitheātrum p. 152

5 On which word in Grumio's speech 'salvē ... sumus' (lines 4–6) does he thump Clemens?

6 Why does Grumio describe himself and Afer as **amīcissimī** (line 6)?

7 What does Grumio receive in addition to the denarii? Why is he given it? Is he pleased?

in forō pp. 152–3

8 How does Grumio's tone of voice change during his speech 'euge! ... reveniō' (lines 7–9)?

9 Why do you think he runs away (line 11)?

10 In line 15 the bakers and the merchants are described as **īrātī**. How do they show this in the rest of this scene?

in culīnā p. 153

11 What state is Grumio's toga in now? What was it like at the beginning of the play?

12 How do you think the merchants say the word **fortis** (line 5) when they see Grumio in the forum?

13 Where had Grumio obtained the denarii which the merchants seized from him? (The answer is in **prope amphitheātrum**.)

14 In what way has Poppaea changed? Can you suggest a reason?

15 Do you feel sorry for Grumio at the end of the play? Give a reason.

Check

Practising the language p. 155

These exercises revise important language points and should be written out.

Ex. 1   This exercise tests your knowledge of verb endings.

Check

If necessary, re-read the language note on p. 136.

Ex. 2   This exercise tests your knowledge of the nominative and accusative, singular and plural.

Check

If you have made more than one wrong choice, revise the forms and uses of these cases on p. 180.

Local government quiz

The following services are needed in nearly every community. Who was responsible for them in Pompeii and who is responsible for them in your town or district today? Fill in the table below. You may need to re-read p. 156.

Service	Pompeii	Your town or district
Trying cases in court		
Water supply		
Markets		
Police force		
Schools (see the background section of Stage 10 if necessary)		
Entertainments (see the background sections of Stages 5 and 8, if necessary)		
Supervising the spending of taxpayers' money		

In what ways are the two lists different? Can you think why? *Check*

Vocabulary checklist 11 p. 160

Learn the checklist.

1 What happens at a *convention*?

2 Why is the *Incredible* Hulk incredible?

3 What can't you do to *illegible* handwriting?

4 If somebody is famous for *liberality*, what sort of person is he or she?

5 Where would you find a *mural* painting?

6 Why is the *Prime* Minister so called?

7 *Captive* and *captivate* are both linked with **capit**. What is the connection?

8 What is a *civil* war?

9 What is a *valedictory* speech?

10 What do you mean when you say that a sound *reverberates* in an empty room?

Check

Language test

1 Turn these sentences into questions by adding a question word from the box. Then translate your questions. Use each question word only once. Do not forget to add a question mark.

> | cūr | ubi | -ne | quid | quis |

a tū recitās.

b servī coquunt.

c rhētor docet.

d virī scrībunt.

e fābulam nārrat.

2 Complete these sentences with the correct word and then translate the sentence.

a senex _____ gladium dedit.
(frātrī, frātrem)

b cīvēs _____ nōn crēdēbant.
(candidātīs, candidātōs)

c vir _____ dōnum prōmīsit.
(uxōrem, uxōrī)

d pater meus _____ semper favēbat.
(mercātōribus, mercātōrēs)

Check

Revision

pp. 186–7   *Word order*

Study paragraphs 1 and 2 and do the examples in paragraph 3 in your head. (You will not be able to do the **Further examples** in paragraph 4 until Stage 12.) Study paragraph 5 and write out a translation of the **Further examples** in paragraph 6.

p. 188   *Longer sentences with* **postquam** *and* **quod**

Study paragraphs 1 and 2; in paragraph 3 translate the first example in each pair in your head; then write out a translation of the second example.

Check

Progress record

Textbook pp. 145–60   Student Study Book pp. 64–70

Stage 11 candidātī	Done	Revised	Any problems?
Local government and elections			
Model sentences			
Marcus et Quārtus			
Local government and elections continued			
About the language 1			
Sulla			
About the language 2			
Lūcius Spurius Pompōniānus: in vīllā			
prope amphitheātrum			
in forō			
in culīnā			
Practising the language			
Local government quiz			
Vocabulary checklist 11			
Language test			
Revision			

Stage 12 Vesuvius

The final Stage of Book I describes the eruption of Vesuvius in AD 79 which destroyed the town of Pompeii. You will read how its people, like those of other places nearby, suffered terror, injury and death.

Picture p. 161

Here people are fleeing from an eruption of Vesuvius in 1779, 1700 years after the eruption that engulfed Pompeii. The volcano was very active from 1631 until its last eruption in 1944.

Model sentences pp. 162–3

1   In these sentences the people are all characters whom you met in earlier Stages. Test your memory of them by filling in the table below.

   a   List the people.

   b   Give their occupation if they have one.

   c   Write a sentence describing what they did in previous stories. The first one is done for you.

Name	Occupation	Description
Syphax	slave-dealer	He sold Melissa to Caecilius / He gave the unlucky Egyptian ring to the innkeeper.

Check

2 Study the **Model sentences**. Here are two new words; you should be able to guess the others.

nūbem	*cloud*	cinerem	*ash*

After working out the meaning, you will see that the various characters are speaking of their worries and sharing their recent experiences.

The arrows on the plan below indicate the place where the characters were when they became aware of the first signs of the eruption. Put their names in the appropriate boxes and say what experiences they had. One is done for you.

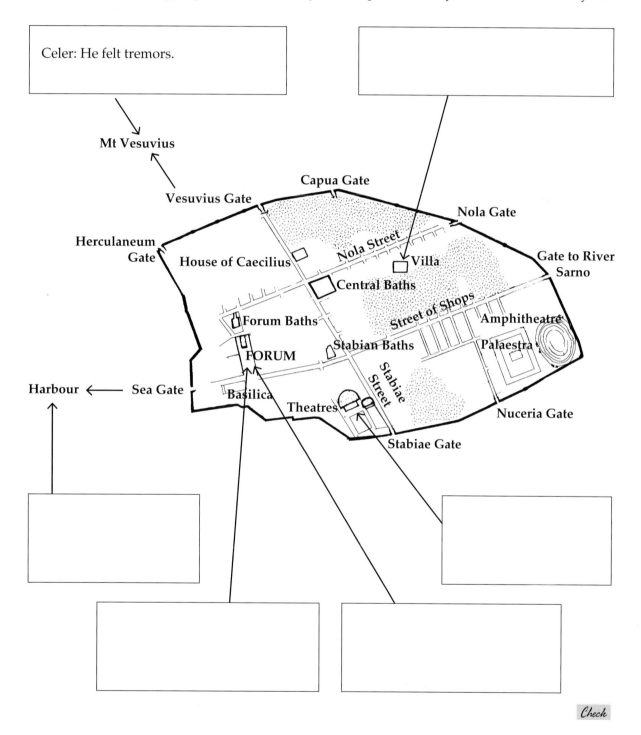

Celer: He felt tremors.

tremōrēs pp. 164–5

Read the story. Work out the meaning of lines 1–12 and answer questions 1–5 on p. 165.

Now read the rest of the story and write out the answers to questions 6–10. Make sure that you include all the relevant points.

Check

Pictures pp. 164–5

It is thought that Caecilius may have decorated his lararium with these reliefs as a thank offering for his survival in the earthquake of AD 62.

p. 164   This panel shows a scene that would have been visible from Caecilius' front door. From left: the water reservoir that supplied the street fountains, public baths and some private houses; the Vesuvius Gate; a stretch of city wall with a cart drawn by two mules.

p. 165   You have seen this panel before. Can you identify the place in Pompeii and the buildings? *Check*

The small figure of the lar is holding a shallow bowl for drink offerings in one hand and a drinking horn in the other. The lares were thought to ensure that the family had plenty to eat and drink.

ad urbem p. 166

Read the story. Work out the meaning of lines 1–13 and answer the questions below. There is no need to write out the answers. If you are in a group, you could divide up the questions and give the answers in turn.

1   Why had Caecilius sent Clemens to the farm? Give TWO reasons.
2   What interrupted Clemens' work at the farm?
3   Where did Clemens go after leaving the farm?
4   Who went with him?
5   Mention THREE things that Clemens saw or heard in the city.
6   Which aspect of the scene would have made most impact on you, if you had been there? Give your reason.
7   Why had Clemens come to find Caecilius at Iulius' house?
8   Where was Iulius' house (see p. 164, lines 1–2)? Look at the plan of Pompeii on p. 73 of this book and suggest or mark in the route through the town which Clemens might have taken from Caecilius' house.

Now read the rest of the story and write out the answers to the questions below. If you are working with others in a group, it would be useful to discuss and compare your answers when you have finished.

9   Where was Holconius going? What do you think his plans were?
10   Judging from his behaviour here, what sort of person would you say Holconius was?
11   Look back at the story in Stage 11 on p. 151, line 7, and then suggest why Caecilius would be especially upset and angry at Holconius' attitude.

Check

The destruction and excavation of Pompeii pp. 172–5

In the stories you have just read, you have seen the effect of the eruption of Vesuvius on the people of Pompeii. Archaeologists have slowly, over the years, gathered evidence and pieced together the past history of the town and the area around.

Read pp. 172–5 and study the pictures to find out more about these discoveries and then answer the questions.

Date	Knowledge of site	Conclusion drawn	Understanding the evidence
After AD 79	None. Town hidden under new soil layer.	None.	None.
Middle Ages			
1594			
1748–1763			
19th century			

1 Fill in this 'discovery record' to show how the town of Pompeii was 'lost' and 'found'. Say what conclusions were drawn by the people of the time and give your opinion of their understanding of the evidence. The first section has been done for you.

2 Write down what conclusions you think you might arrive at if you found the following in Pompeii:

   a a table with food on it;

   b a room containing a box with a large number of coins in;

   c the remains of lead piping in a garden;

   d the skeleton of a young woman showing signs of overwork;

   e lines of hollow spaces in the ash in open ground;

   f a lantern surrounded by bones (see p. 176).

Check

About the language pp. 170–1

Read the information and learn the new forms of the imperfect and perfect tenses shown in paragraphs 2 and 3. Learn the new forms in paragraph 4 and translate the examples in paragraph 5 without looking at the tables.

tū	mercātor	nōs
puerī	ego	vōs

Further exercise   Choosing from the pool, fill in the spaces with the correct word. Then translate the sentences.

You will not need all the words from the pool.

a _____ docēbāmus.

b _____ portāvī.

c _____ ambulāvistī.

d _____ erant laetī.

e _____ audiēbātis.

Check

Pictures p. 171

Top In the eruption the whole of the top of the mountain was blown off.

The figure partly visible on the left is Bacchus, the god of wine, dressed in grapes.

Middle left and bottom The remains of the old cone can be seen with the new cone rising within it. Vesuvius is now overdue for an eruption and the Italian government has drawn up plans to evacuate the highly populated area.

ad vīllam p. 167

Read the story together with the following translation for lines 1–11.

In the city there was very great panic. Ash was now falling thicker. Flames were everywhere. After they entered the city, Caecilius and his friends began to make for the house. But progress was difficult, because many Pompeians were filling the streets. However, Caecilius was hurrying bravely through the streets.

The cloud was now very thick. Suddenly Iulius cried out, 'You hurry to the house. I do not feel well.'

At once he fell down to the ground unconscious. Clemens carried Iulius to the nearest temple.

'You have done very well', Caecilius said to his slave. 'You have saved Iulius. I promise you your freedom.'

Continue the translation for lines 12–19 by filling in the spaces.

Then Caecilius left _____ and _____ to the house. Clemens _____ with Iulius in the _____ . _____ Iulius recovered consciousness. 'Where _____ ?' he asked. '_____ safe', the slave answered Iulius. '_____ Isis has _____ _____ . After _____ fell down on the ground, _____ _____ to this temple.'

'I thank you very much, because _____ saved me', said Iulius. 'But _____ is Caecilius?'

Read to the end of the story. What do Iulius and Clemens finally decide to do? Which of them do you think made the better decision? Why?

Check

fīnis p. 168

Read the story and then write out an English translation of lines 1–9.

Now read lines 10–26 to find out what happened to Caecilius and his family. Answer the questions, which are designed to be a quick check of your understanding of the story. The answers need not be written out and, if you are in a group, you could do them together orally.

1 Where was Caecilius lying?

2 Why was he so badly injured?

3 What did Caecilius tell Clemens about Metella and Quintus (lines 14–18)? What did he think had happened to them?

4 What did he tell Clemens to do (line 17)?

5 Why did Clemens at first refuse?

6 What did Caecilius say to Clemens about Quintus (lines 21–2)?

7 When did Clemens finally obey Caecilius?

8 Why is the final action of Cerberus described as **frūstrā**?

9 What do you think will happen to Clemens now?

Check

Vocabulary checklist 12 p. 176

Learn the checklist. In the table below, a number of word descriptions have been given to you. From the pool of English words below the table, choose the correct word for each description. Then write down the Latin word with which the English word is connected in meaning. Put down the meaning of the Latin word.

Word description	English word	Latin word	Meaning
A person who runs away			
Not existing on Earth			
Finish			
Being the only one of its kind			
Unpleasant heat and redness of a part of the body			
A feeling of not having achieved one's aim			
Land that is almost an island			
Lying near to something			

extraterrestrial	frustration	adjacent	complete
inflammation	unique	peninsula	fugitive

Check

Language test

1 Tick the correct word in brackets and translate the completed sentences.

   a multī cīvēs ex urbe celeriter _____. (discessimus, discessistis, discessērunt)

   b vōs viās _____. (complēbāmus, complēbātis, complēbant)

   c tandem tū ad fundum _____. (vēnī, vēnistī, vēnit)

   d ego ad montem herī _____. (ambulāvī, ambulāvistī, ambulāvit)

   e nōs ad templum _____. (fugiēbāmus, fugiēbātis, fugiēbant)

   f ego _____ sollicitus. (eram, erās, erat)

2 Look at each of these sentences. Decide which tense the verb is in and write the sentence in the appropriate column in the table. Translate the sentences into English. The first one is done for you.

   a canis dominum custōdit.   d uxōrem frūstrā quaerēbam.

   b epistulam ad frātrem mīsī.   e in triclīniō dormiēbātis.

   c tremōrēs sentiō.   f tūne pecūniam cēpistī?

Tense	Latin sentence	Translation
Present	canis dominum custōdit.	The dog is guarding his master.
Present		
Imperfect		
Imperfect		
Perfect		
Perfect		

Check

Revision

pp. 182–4 *Verbs*

Study paragraphs 1–4. In paragraphs 3 and 4 you will find that the verbs in the tables have been divided into four groups or conjugations. Make a note of the differences between the conjugations in the present, imperfect and perfect tenses.

Paragraph 5 Write out the answers to the exercise.

Paragraph 6 Without looking at the table write out a translation of examples **a–d**. Before translating examples **e–h** study paragraph 2 again. Use a variety of meanings for the present, imperfect and perfect tenses.

Paragraph 7 Study and learn the present and imperfect forms.

p. 185 *Ways of forming the perfect tense*

Study paragraphs 1 and 2 and learn the present and perfect forms of these common verbs.

pp. 186–7 *Word order*

Read again paragraphs 1–3 and write out the examples in paragraph 4. *Check*

Progress record   Textbook pp. 161–76   Student Study Book pp. 72–8

Stage 12 Vesuvius	Done	Revised	Any problems?
Model sentences			
tremōrēs			
ad urbem			
The destruction and excavation of Pompeii			
About the language			
ad vīllam			
fīnis			
Vocabulary checklist 12			
Language test			
Revision			

Short guide to the pronunciation of Latin

Short vowels

a   as in English 'aha'

e   as in English 'pet'

i   as in English 'dip'

o   as in English 'pot'

u   as in English 'put'

y   as in French 'plume'

Long vowels (marked as follows)

ā   as in English 'father'

ē   as in French 'fianc**ée**'

ī   as in English 'd**ee**p'

ō   as in French 'b**eau**' (roughly as in English 'c**oa**t')

ū   as in English 'f**oo**l' (not as in 'm**u**sic')

Diphthongs (two vowels sounded together in a single syllable)

ae as in English 'high'

au as in English 'h**ow**'

ei as in English 'd**ay**'

eu no exact English equivalent: 'e' is combined with 'oo' (not as in 'f**ew**')

oe as in English 'b**oy**'

ui no exact English equivalent: 'u' is combined with 'i'

Consonants

b   (usually) as in English 'big'

b   (followed by t or s) as in English 'li**ps**'

c   as in English 'cat' or 'king' (not as in 'centre' or 'cello')

ch as in English 'cat' pronounced with emphasis (not as in 'chin')

g   as in English 'got' (not as in 'gentle')

gn as 'ngn' in English 'hangnail'

i   (before a vowel and sometimes written as j) as in English 'you'

n   (usually) as in English 'net'

n   (before c, g or qu) as in English 'anger'

ph as in English 'pig' pronounced with emphasis (not as in 'photo')

qu as in English 'quick'

r   as Scottish ('rolled') r in 'bird'

s   as in English 'sing' (not as in 'roses')

th as in English 'terrible' pronounced with emphasis (not as in 'the' or 'theatre')

v   (often written as u) as in English 'wind'

x   as in English 'box'

Other consonants are pronounced as in English.

Double consonants

ll as in English 'hall-light' (not as in 'taller')

nn as in English 'thin-nosed' (not as in 'dinner')

pp as in English 'hip-pocket' (not as in 'happy')

Word stress (indicated in this section by *italic* print)

In spoken Latin a syllable in each word is stressed. The following are the general rules for deciding where the stress should fall:

1   In a word of two syllables, the stress is on the first syllable, e.g. m*ā*ter, c*o*quus.

2   In a word of more than two syllables,

   a) the stress falls on the second syllable from the end if that syllable contains a long vowel, or a short vowel followed by two consonants, e.g. sal*ū*tat, Met*e*lla;

   b) otherwise the stress falls on the third syllable from the end, e.g. Caec*i*lius, f*u*rcifer, laet*i*ssimus.

Further examples (with stress marked)

am*ī*cus	s*e*det	v*ī*lla
p*ā*vō	l*ae*tus	l*au*dat
qu*o*que	lab*ō*rat	m*a*gnus
i*ā*nua	*ē*heu	v*ī*num
v*e*rberat	qu*ae*rit	*ū*nus